How to Kill an Addict(ion)
Recovery with God

By Michele Eich

"You cannot force people to comprehend a message they are not ready to receive, but never underestimate the power of planting a seed."

Anonymous

Many Thanks

I want to thank my family and friends for loving and supporting me throughout this journey. My children are amazing examples of God's grace, and being their mom is my greatest accomplishment. I am grateful for my husband, Lynn. His unconditional love and support make it possible for me to follow my dreams.

I am grateful to the beautiful souls who are the *Voices of Recovery*. They courageously shared their stories with honesty and humility to encourage others and bring hope to the hurting. My prayer is that many people will read their testimonies and see that all things are possible with God.

I would like to thank Sherry Ward and the entire team at Square Tree Publishing for making this experience positive and enjoyable. They made themselves available to help at any time, and I could not have done this project without them.

Above all, I want to thank Jesus for saving me and transforming my life. Without Him, none of this would have been possible. God has exceeded my every hope, prayer, and dream. He is still in the miracle making business, and I look forward to hearing the testimonies of more people who are set free. They too are the *Voices of Recovery*.

Dedication

I dedicate this book to BRAT with much love and gratitude.

Table of Contents

○-○

Introduction

This book contains truths that have the power to set captives free. It is not because of what I can do, but because of what God already did. Many people probably want to know why I am writing such a book. For starters, I have a license of practical ministry; I am a certified growth coach, and I was a teacher for over 20 years. I also consider myself a "fool for Christ," which trumps all of my previous qualifications infinitely. Above all, I have been set free from my own addiction. It wasn't to drugs, alcohol, or any other substance. It was to a person, and it almost destroyed my life and the lives of others. More on that later.

Addictions can come in many forms. I prefer to call them "life-controlling issues," and most people have them. We can be controlled by various substances, people, negative thoughts, food, destructive habits, and more. We are hearing stories of lives ruined every day, and more must be done to help those who are struggling. My focus is what has already been done to solve the problems we face. The question we should be asking ourselves is this: *Did Jesus provide a way out or not?* I believe He did, and it is not just for the "sweet by and by," but the rough "here and now."

I recently saw a quote that read, "The world is waiting for you to become all God created you to be." With our current state of affairs, we need all hands on deck. Parents are burying their children and raising their grandbabies. Our streets are full of needles and addicts with nowhere to go. Our prisons are overflowing with people who need help. Our systems are designed to punish people, for the most part, but punishment never transformed anyone from the inside out. It is time we all do our part to help this growing epidemic. Before I could write this book, however, I had to get to a place in my own journey that would allow me to be honest and transparent before the world. In doing so, I am taking some risks, but I believe that it is worth it. If I am helping one person find freedom, then I will celebrate that throughout all eternity. I am not perfect by any means, but thankfully Jesus is. By following Him, I have found new life, and it is glorious.

One of my favorite parts about this book is called "Voices of Recovery" which contains testimonies of real people who have overcome a multitude of life-controlling issues. They were able to accomplish this because they invited God into their journey, and that was a game-changer. Jesus helped these beautiful people get out of the mess that they found themselves in, and I share their stories to show you what is possible. I know these individuals personally, and I am happy to introduce them and showcase their amazing experiences with you. Each chapter in the book ends with a testimony from these overcomers, and I think you will find them incredibly uplifting. I certainly do!

When we are stuck, we need encouragement from compassionate individuals who know what it is like to be in a place that seems hopeless. I am reminded of the story of the man who fell into a sewer. He could see people walking above him, but they passed by without really taking notice. A pastor walked by and dropped the man a note that said he was praying for him. Later a police officer warned him of criminals in the area. A nice lady tossed down a $5 bill and told him to "Hang in there."

Full of despair, the man stuck in the bowels of the city was about to give up. Just when he thought all hope was lost, his best friend jumped in the hole with him. The man said, "Why did you do that? Now we're both stuck!"

To that his friend replied, "Don't worry. I once fell down this sewer, and I know the way out."

I want to emphasize that one person cannot fix another. What we can do is point others to Jesus, who can get the job done. He is the one who jumped down into the "sewer" for us. He came into a lost and dying world to proclaim freedom to the captives. Maybe you believe in Him, and maybe you don't. I am hopeful that after reading this book you will see that He knows the way out of your situation. If you follow Him, you can access the freedom and abundant life He came to give you. I am living proof that it is possible.

If you are the way I was about 25 years ago, you may be wondering how in the world that could possibly happen. The good news is that you don't have to figure out how, but just keep trusting that it will come to pass. Your mess wasn't made overnight, and it won't be fixed in a day, but just keep swimming, my friend. These waters are warm and friendly.

You may find this book helpful if these statements apply to you:
- You want to get well.
- You are sick and tired of being sick and tired.
- You are open to trusting God.
- You have tried to break free, but nothing has worked.
- You have even the smallest shred of hope God can help you.

This book may not be a great fit for you if these statements apply to you:
- You want a quick fix.
- You don't really want to get better.
- You expect someone else to do it for you.
- You refuse to take any responsibility for your circumstances.
- You are completely closed off to God.

After God unraveled my mess, I spent six years teaching people who had life-controlling issues at a place called The Farm. During that time, I learned a lot about these beautiful souls, myself, and God. The lessons in this book are a compilation of teachings I did there. I would love it if you would join me on this journey. I know the One who says that all things are possible with Him.

I wrote this book primarily for Christians who are stuck. It is not only for people with addictions, but I would guess that most of us are controlled by something or someone. Maybe you have a bad habit that you would like to get rid of, or you are just feeling stuck in life. This book could help with those issues as well.

When it comes to past mistakes, believers in Jesus can get overwhelmed with guilt, shame, and condemnation. These can destroy a person and make them feel worthless and hopeless. The good news is that there is no condemnation for those who are in Christ. Jesus's blood has cleansed us from our guilty consciences. He has taken our shame and replaced it with freedom.

If you don't know Jesus yet, then I pray that you will invite Him into your journey even if it looks quite messy right now. He is not afraid of a fight, a mess, or anything else you're dealing with. He is waiting to roll up His sleeves and jump right in there with you. I am thankful that you are open to trusting Him!

Before we go any further, let's pray. *Father, I thank You for this opportunity to share your love, goodness, and power with others. I can sense that someone reading this is ashamed of his/her issue, but I ask that You would graciously reassure that person that he/she is deeply loved by You. I believe You have been waiting for the readers of this book to invite You into their journey. You are not intimidated by our messes or struggles, but You are excited to jump in and help us clean them up. We need You, God. In our own power we are weak, but You are strong and able to do exceedingly, abundantly more than we can ask or even fathom. Please surround the readers of this book with angelic activity and your precious Holy Spirit as they begin a journey of new life in You. Amen.*

Insanity Defined

You have probably heard the definition of insanity. It is doing the same thing over and over and expecting different results. There is a great story in the Bible that illustrates this concept. You can find it in John 5 when Jesus meets an invalid at the pool of Bethsaida. This poor soul had been coming to the pool for 38 years. The people believed that angels stirred the water, and the first ones to get in would be healed.

Did you catch the part where he was there for 38 years? The man was coming down to the water for almost four decades in hopes of getting healed, and nothing changed. This time was going to be different though. The invalid met Jesus that day, and He asked this man one of the most powerful questions that has ever been asked. *Do you want to get well?* Boom, there it is. Instead of answering yes or no, the man began to make excuses that no one would take him down to the water, again for 38 years!

I want to stop right here and say one thing that will really keep people stuck is blame. This man's first response was that his friends didn't come through for him. When you refuse to take responsibility for the things that happen, you have nothing left but to blame others for your lot in life. Did others play a part in what happened to us? Absolutely. However, blaming people and waiting for them to change or own their mistakes will keep us from moving forward in our own life.

I see the blame game being played out all the time. Here are some examples:

> • A man failed a drug test, but it was his boss's fault for ordering a "random" in the first place.

> • Child Protective Services has been contacted because a woman had neglected her children, but it is the teacher's fault for reporting it.

> • A man got caught drinking on the job, but it was his supervisor's fault for creating such a stressful workplace.

> • A woman got fired from her job for being late to work so many times, but it wasn't really her fault because no one would give her a ride to work, even though she spent her bus fare at the casino.

The enemy entices us to blame others because when we do, we don't have to change or seek forgiveness. Why? We've done nothing wrong. It is everyone else's problem.

The enemy will encourage us to blame others and even God for what has happened to us or through us. If he can get us to blame God, then naturally we would never go to Him for help. Blame is a sticky quagmire and an easy trap to fall into because we don't have to take responsibility for anything as long as it is someone else's fault. Again, this is a recipe for staying stuck. Don't take the bait!

I don't want to offend people out of the gate, but this is a big lesson to learn from the invalid in this story. Taking ownership for our own lives and mistakes is HARD. Our mind has certain self-protective techniques like blame so that we don't have to own our stuff and make changes. Taking responsibility for our part in whatever happened can be very difficult.

It would be much easier to blame others, the devil, the world, bad luck, or that the sun was in our eyes. Blame says that others must change. Taking responsibility says that you will change. It is an empowering mind shift that needs to happen in order to move forward. If you continue to blame, you'll stay stuck in a pity party that no one else will want to attend!

At the Pool of Bethsaida, Jesus didn't show the man pity. He could have said, "Oh, you poor fellow! You have some pretty lame friends. I am so sorry no one was here to help you." Nope, that is not what He said at all. Jesus simply asked the man if he wanted to get well. We can assume that he did since this man had been coming to the pool for, did I mention, 38 years! However, the man started with an excuse and basically blamed his friends for not getting him to the angelic waters quick enough. Well, there's always tomorrow!

Jesus simply told the man to pick up his mat and walk. No pity party, no fanfare, just a command to get the mat and go. Please note that Jesus did not say, "Hey, let me get that for you!" Nope, He told the man to pick it up and move forward into his future. This is significant, and it is probably not because Jesus didn't want to touch a mat/rug that a man had been lying on for almost 40 years without a good dry cleaning!

I believe Jesus was leading the man to pick up his mat because He wanted the invalid to take *responsibility* for his part in whatever put him there in the first place. It is an act of faith in response to Jesus's command. When we can stop blaming other people or situations and take responsibility for our part in what got us stuck, we have just taken the first step in recovery.

I realize that people played a role in you getting stuck, and I am not trying to be insensitive to that fact at all. I have had similar experiences as others did things that contributed to my choices. Even though others were involved, it is my responsibility to move forward. Yes, this and that happened, but what am I going to do about it now? This quote sums it up perfectly: "Your wound may not have been your fault, but your healing is your responsibility."

If I am waiting for an apology, it will probably happen on the 12th day of never. If I am waiting for others to own up to their mistakes or step up and do their part, it may not happen. If I am waiting by the waters for my friends to take me down to the healing pool, I could remain stuck for years. We cannot control what others do or not do, but we can control our reactions and decide what we are going to do about it. This is called taking your power back.

The Bible says that the man was an "invalid." This word is defined as a person made weak or disabled by illness or injury. So let me ask you this: What exactly was wrong with this man? Did he have a disease? Was he addicted to something? Was it inherited from his parents? Was it contagious? Did he sustain a life-changing injury? The Bible doesn't tell us, and do you know why? Because it is not as important as Jesus healing him from whatever kept him stuck. Read that again.

We have to be careful not to major in the minors. I have heard people question whether life-controlling issues or addictions are inherited, caught, taught, or an actual disease. We could argue this until the cows come home, but it will not help anyone. We don't know exactly what caused the man by the pool to be stuck there for so long, but we can clearly see how he got unstuck. He met a man named Jesus, picked up his mat, and walked away healed and whole. Kaboom!

Getting lost in the weeds about whether the problem is a disease or choice will take us nowhere fast. However, focusing on Jesus will definitely help us walk in wholeness just like the invalid experienced. This book will not focus on problems as much as it will discuss solutions. In fact, there is One solution, and He is Jesus. Whatever your struggle, He has the answer, and He is the answer!

I don't know what you have tried in order to break free from every chain that binds you. I can only imagine the time, resources, money, and more that have been spent for you to find freedom. We often come to Jesus as a last resort, but that is not a reason to beat yourself up. The fact that you are reading this book tells me (and God) that you are ready to make some serious changes to move forward in your life. Go ahead; pick up your mat and follow Him. This is the first step to freedom.

Voices of Recovery Presents
Rusty

Growing up in small town America, I never imagined I would wake up one day to find myself an addicted, homeless bum. But at age 19, I did. The first 19 years of my life were pretty decent. I grew up going to church with my hardworking parents and brother. We had what we needed, and life was pretty good. Even though I went to church, I only knew the rules-based, 'religious' Jesus. I didn't feel like I lived up to those standards, so I threw in the towel on God.

I became the youngest licensed Private Investigator in the country at age 18 and was flourishing in my military role. It was exactly what I had hoped for. What I didn't anticipate was a cocaine addiction gripping my life. What started as a hobby to take away the pain on the days I felt lonely and empty turned into a hurricane of bad decisions.

Within a short time, I lost everything. I was homeless, jobless, friendless, and went on to make some terrible decisions. Eventually I found myself in cell 121. While I was incarcerated, a gentleman with the Gideons would come visit me. He was in his 90s. Even though he wasn't a very exciting speaker (he would actually fall asleep while talking to me occasionally), it wasn't what he said that made a difference. It's what he did.

He showed up every Sunday, and his commitment showed me that God wasn't done with me yet and that someone still believed in Rusty Boruff. In cell 121, I accepted Christ. Even though I was still behind bars for nearly a year, it was one of the best years of my life.

One of the things I learned in that cell is that some of the toughest moments of your life can become a catalyst for what God has for you. My dream was to start a place for people like me who were getting out of jail and needed support.

A few years later, as a felon and with absolutely no resources, God made a way. Today, that dream is called One Eighty. We are a nationally recognized non-profit leading the way in reaching kids prior to addiction, ministering to broken neighborhoods, and restoring lives of those in crisis, poverty, or addiction.

Rusty Boruff
OneEighty.org

Stupid Questions

When I was teaching, I would often say that there is no such thing as a stupid question. Well, I was wrong. I've heard a few "dandies" in my life (especially from middle schoolers) and have probably asked a few myself.

Let's go back to Jesus's question from John 5. He asked, "Do you want to get well?" On the surface, that seems like a really stupid question. After all, who doesn't want to get well? Why would Jesus ask such a seemingly stupid question? Sometimes Jesus will ask us something, not because He needs to know, but we need to know how we'll respond to what He is offering.

This is one of the most straightforward and powerful questions that He can ask someone who is bound with something. I know a lot of people who *don't* want to get well. Some of them are unaware that they can, and once people see that recovery is possible, others still don't want it. You may be asking, "Why in the world would someone not want to get well?" Great question and I am glad you asked!

At the risk of offending someone, I am going to tell you one reason why people *don't* want to get well. Are you ready? Their illness gives them attention. Say what? Yep, that is the truth. This obviously doesn't apply to everyone, and I am hoping and praying it doesn't apply to you, so bear with me, please.

Imagine someone crying out on social media about all her problems. Posts can be summed up as, "Woe is me." Then picture someone private messaging that person with a possible solution. *Crickets* Then further posts about how no one loves her; life is hopeless; no one really cares, etc. This individual has no real interest in getting well and loves the attention that the issue is providing.

Whether or not someone responds to our cries for help, I know that there is One who cares, and He is Jesus. I now recognize that He is my source. Jesus is the missing *piece* from my life. Jesus is the missing *peace* my heart desires. Before I met the Lord and really got to know Him, I tried to fill the void in my life with people. I sought attention from them because I mistakenly thought that they could meet my need for self-worth.

Because of the rejection I experienced as a child, I would gravitate toward men to meet my needs. I literally craved attention from the opposite sex, and it doesn't take a rocket scientist to figure out how a young woman can get men to notice her. This led me into heartache, chaos, more rejection, and eventually an earth-shattering event that nearly destroyed my life. I will be sharing more about this later in the book.

When we know the love of Jesus, we are secure. His eyes are *always* on us. Jesus is a loving and attentive Father who adores His children. When we experience His unconditional love for us, we don't need attention from the world to make us feel valued. When He asks us if we want to get well, we can shout, "Yes!"

If we don't know Him and His love, however, then we open ourselves up to looking for affirmation from a fickle world. Think of movie stars who have the "love" and adoration from fans, and then look at their lives once the music fades. We could all name several who crashed and burned after the world found someone else to applaud.

I have seen many people who don't want to get well. They like the attention, drama, and trauma that their situation brings. It is very difficult to help these individuals. Their affliction serves a purpose which is giving them attention that is only false love. Until they find real love, they will continue to stay stuck in their messes.

Others don't want to get well because they fear the

unknown. Getting well means changes will take place, and some do not welcome this. It means that they will have a brand-new life with a variety of new options and choices before them. That can be terrifying. As far as the invalid was concerned, he really didn't have to wake up and decide what to do on a particular day. He knew that he would be going to the Pool of Bethsaida. There were no goals, hopes, dreams, aspirations, or anything like that.

Once the man became whole, he had options. He had to make decisions, and those can be terrifying, especially for someone stuck for so long. I am sure he was overjoyed to be free from whatever kept him bound, but he probably felt a bit overwhelmed with all the choices he had to make. Some people like their comfort zone so much that they will not move forward into healing for fear of the changes it will bring.

Thankfully, believers have a wonderful Guide sent to do life with them. He is the Holy Spirit, the Comforter, Ever Present Help in Time of Trouble, Counselor, Advocate, Spirit of Wisdom, and much, much more. When we walk with God, He is there every step of the way to lead and guide us into a brilliant future! He says not to fear. Why? Because He is with us.

The third reason many people don't attempt to get well is because the recovery process seems almost impossible. The truth is that it can be very difficult. You know what is also difficult? Staying stuck in a mess. I interviewed a couple recently, and the husband was addicted to pornography. They contemplated divorce many times, and the wife said that they had two mountains in front of them: the mountain of divorce, and the mountain of working on their marriage. She added there is no easy way out. Both mountains are tough to tackle, but the view from the peak of the healing their marriage mountain is so majestically beautiful and definitely worth the climb! I love this imagery so much. With God on our journey, recovery is not necessarily easy, but it is possible, and it has a happy ending as an added bonus!

I want to address this not-so-stupid question right out of the gate in hopes that the answer will be yes. If it is no, then there is honestly no sense wasting time with conversations about getting well. Your "yes" will prepare your heart to receive and to move forward with Jesus. You can pick up your mat and take the next steps with Him.

So here goes: *Do you want to get well?* If you do, then keep reading. I have so much to share with you!

Voices of Recovery Presents

Jenny

I grew up in the Upper Peninsula of Michigan. My mom was a raging alcoholic, and my dad was a workaholic. I was the second to last child of six kids. My parents got divorced twice and remarried twice to each other. It was a very scary house to live in. My dad was an atheist, so I knew nothing about God.

When I was about nine years old, I was very suicidal. All I could think about was how could I die to get away from this life. I wanted to find a semi-truck to jump in front of, but I lived in the neighborhood and couldn't find my way to the highway. I had no self-esteem. I was depressed, angry, violent, and did not want to live anymore.

When I was around 10 my brother smoked pot with me. My first thought was if I can stay feeling like this for the rest of my life, maybe I won't kill myself. From then on, all I could think about was getting high to stop feeling all the horrible feelings I felt. By the time I was in high school, I was dealing drugs and getting high before school, during school, and after school.

When my dad was home, I felt safe because my dad told my mom if she beat the kids, he would beat her. My dad had a heart attack and died one week before I turned 18. About a month after that, my mom kicked me out of the house, and things went from bad to worse very fast! My oldest brother was a drug dealer, and that's when I was introduced to cocaine. When I was 20 years old, I got busted for a delivery of cocaine and possession of marijuana. I was facing 5 to 20 years in prison.

My probation officer told me I should go to treatment. I had no idea what treatment was! I was in really bad shape. I was about 110 pounds, and I had an ulcer in my stomach that hurt all the time. My mouth also hurt all the time from using cocaine every day. I felt worthless. I was angry and very paranoid, so I went to treatment. While there, I did not use for two weeks, and that was about the longest I had been clean and sober in many, many years.

I had no idea what it was like to be clean and sober and didn't understand it at all. I was very angry and frustrated and extremely confused! I said out loud, "I don't know You God, but I can't handle this anymore!! I don't understand anything about this being clean and sober stuff. If I don't get it today, I will find my way to the roof of this hospital and I will jump off!" God knew I was not kidding. Suicidal thoughts were extremely normal to me, and I was more than ready to die. I did not know what it was like to be happy anymore, and I just could not handle life. That day we had a speaker. He was an older gentleman, and he talked about how he was in an insane asylum many years ago when he was in his 40s. He talked about 'wet brain' which can happen with some alcoholics. As he spoke, I heard somebody speak to me and say, "That is going to be you."

I looked around in shock. I noticed nobody was talking to me. I knew it was God! That pierced my heart so hard I don't know if I can put it into words. All I know was at that moment my desire to drink and do drugs went away. I never drank or did any kind of drug since then, and a desire to live came into my heart. It was a feeling I never remember feeling before. It was the first time in many years I felt hope and thought maybe I might feel some happiness in my life.

After my time in treatment, I went to court and got sentenced to six months in jail for possession of marijuana and lifetime probation for delivery of cocaine. The day I got out of jail I was able to get into a long-term Treatment Center for 12 months. It was a very intense treatment center. It dealt a lot about feelings about how to deal with life without drinking and drugging. My brother and his wife lived in lower Michigan and took me in. I started to think about if God was real. I started going to a church and began dating someone. After a little while he broke up with me because he wanted to pursue the lifestyle of drinking and drugging.

I was so hurt that I did not want to date another guy that had anything to do with God. At that point I was very angry with God. I questioned if He was real and didn't want to have any more to do with Him. I no longer believed in anything the Bible had to say. I met a guy named Mike who was 21, and I was 23. He went to church when he was younger but didn't go any more, and we never really discussed why he stopped going to church. I was just happy he didn't go.

We got married a few years after that, and we had two incredible daughters, Kaylyn and Ashley. As time went on, I felt a lot of anger and unforgiveness even though I had been clean and sober for many years. I was acting like my mother, somebody I did not want to be like at all, but I didn't know how to stop. My marriage was starting to fall apart. My life was starting to fall apart, but I had no idea how to put it back together. I didn't know how to stop all the anger, and it was ruining my life. I didn't realize that it was Satan. I had no belief in Satan or God. All I knew was my heart felt extremely hard, and I did not know what to do.

My husband turned 37 in June of 2007. One week later, he came home from work and wasn't feeling well. We didn't know he had a torn aorta. Within 15 minutes of him being at home, he died basically right in front of me and my children. I called 911 as my daughter paced back and forth and said, "Please Daddy please Daddy, don't die!!!" The paramedics worked on him for a long time with no success.

My two children were six years and ten years old at the time. My life completely changed in a matter of minutes. I was now widowed with two children and in total shock. The thought of living my life without my husband, and my children never having a dad to be there for them for all of the important things in their lives, was devastating! My boss was very generous and gave me a month off with pay. That gave me time to think. I knew from my time in treatment that if I didn't process these feelings, I would start using drugs again, and I sure didn't want to do that!

As I looked at my children, I could not imagine putting my kids through what I went through as a child. That's when I cried out to God and said, "I don't know You, but I'm going to give You a shot because I don't know what else to do." At that point I surrendered my life to Jesus Christ. I started to read the Bible, which I had never done. My life started to change. After a few months I noticed my heart was not hard anymore. I did not understand how that could happen so fast. I had emotional healing in my life even from the past. I can't explain how that happened.

I started to forgive people like my brother whom I hadn't talked to for five years. I started to care about people and have compassion for them. My heart was coming alive. I was being the parent to my children that God wanted me to be. I was taking care of things. Even as a single mom, God was there for me giving me strength and hope that I have never known. He was doing things in my life that I couldn't even imagine!! I have been through some extremely hard times and God has been there for me and gotten me through every time!

I went back to court a few months ago and got the delivery of cocaine expunged off my record. God is so, so good! It's been 12 years since my husband died, and I have been clean and sober for 31 years now. God has given me more hope, peace, joy, and confidence than I could ever imagine in a lifetime. Jesus has healed me of many emotional traumas. As God reveals to me who I am in Jesus Christ, I become more and more like Him. I love Jesus with every fiber of my being!

Because of Jesus Christ, my kids are not growing up like I grew up. Because I chose God, He broke the cycle, and I want people to know there is hope. Ashley is going to college, and Kaylyn is happily married with a baby and works for a vet. Because of all God has done in my life, I'm a better mom, friend, employee, and better person than I ever could have ever imagined. God can take any situation and turn it around for the better. Jesus Christ gives me hope, joy, peace, and the love that I never knew was possible. I'm an amazing child of God because of Jesus Christ!

Jenny Hans

Pebbles and Boulders

If you are reading this, then it most likely means that you answered 'yes' to the question and want to get well. Hooray! I am so excited and encouraged by this. You took a HUGE step into your freedom and destiny by doing so. I am proud of you!

I once heard someone say that when God wants to get your attention, He will first send a pebble. If that doesn't do the trick, He will then send a rock. If you are hardheaded and won't budge, then you will get the boulder. It will certainly get your attention if it doesn't crush you!

Actually, I am not sure if this is true or not, but it does make sense. Look, God is a good, good Father. What does a loving parent do when his/her child is headed for danger? Mom or Dad will give a warning and then appropriate correction to the kid who continually chooses to disobey. God disciplines those He loves. He doesn't want us to be harmed in any way, but we often ignore the warning signs. I sure did.

I used to think that God was the big party pooper in the sky who wanted me to have zero fun. Looking back, I believed that God was real, but I wanted to have my "fun" first before coming to Him. Naturally, I didn't want to go to hell, but my plan was to invite Him into my life when I was old and gray and no longer wanted to have good times anymore.

I have to laugh and even shake my head at this ridiculous line of thinking because God is fun, adventurous, and never boring or dull! Let's face it: I was lost. At the time, I enjoyed my "sin" and ignored the multitude of pebbles God was flinging my way. I eventually got the boulder treatment, and at the time, it was NOT pleasant. Like I said, it almost crushed me, but it was the only thing that got this girl's attention.

As you read the testimonies of those who contributed to the "Voices of Recovery," it doesn't take long to see that many of them also got the "boulder" treatment. Even though it is painful, they are eternally grateful for the wake-up call. Many of them probably had others who tried to lead them to Jesus at some point on their journey. When things are going well, we tend to continue on our way and ignore God. However, when the boulder comes, perhaps we are a little more attentive. We all want a Great Awakening, but first must come the rude awakening! If that is what it takes to get us to listen to God, then I am all for it.

If it took a boulder to get you to wake up and seek God, well thank Him for it! Whatever it takes to get us to see our need for God, it is honestly a blessing in disguise. One of my all-time favorite verses in the Bible is Romans 8:28. It reminds us that God works ALL things together for good for those who love Him and are called according to His purposes. (Still can't see it? Neither could I, but give Him time.)

The "worst" thing that happened in my life (aka boulder) was actually the BEST thing that could have happened. Why? Because it got my attention and kept me from going further down the path that was leading to my destruction. I got a rude awakening and eventually started to seek God for meaning and purpose, which led to me finding the true love I had been looking for all along. His name is Jesus.

Maybe you are reading this from a jail cell. You got the boulder, and it stinks. Perhaps you almost died, and it scared you. If this is what it took to get your attention, then praise God for the boulder! Some of you might have lost important relationships. I've seen it happen countless times, but I have also seen God restore in amazing ways. You may not realize it now, but He has all of eternity to reveal His truths and His ways.

I have seen many people crash and burn as they chase the things of this world. Whether it's drugs, alcohol, sex, pornography, etc., these things are "fun" and exciting for a while, or we wouldn't do them. However, the lives that are destroyed from these chains could fill up many books. God has provided a way out, however, and it is so simple that it is complex. Keep reading to discover that He has already solved your problem even if He had to send that boulder to get you to see it.

Voices of Recovery Presents

Roseanne

The first time I became conscious of being overweight was very early on. I was in third grade and the gym scale said 99 pounds. Only one pound from 100. I was much chubbier than the other children. Not long after that, I was with my parents in a retail furniture store. As I was climbing the escalator to the second floor, I saw my reflection in a mirror, but not knowing it was me until after I said, out loud, "Wow, that girl is UGLY!" When I realized it was me, my heart sank to a deeper level of lack of confidence. Though I grew up in an average American-Italian family, I had no knowledge of God or the Bible; that didn't happen until later, when I became desperate to know why I was on earth and what is this life all about anyway.

During high school I did not date, and I tagged along with cheerleader type friends until I could no longer hang on. I was in school, but decided to start working a lot to bury my pain of being overweight and lack of confidence. To my surprise, I began to get thinner and more noticed by guys. It freaked me out! With this newfound obsession, enjoying that I was feeling better and looking better, I took it to an extreme. I was now struggling with an eating disorder called bulimia as well as developing suicidal thoughts because of fear and depression raging in my life. By now, I was in my first year of college and could not survive. It became overwhelming because I was pushing so hard, could not attain perfection, and was disappointing my parents because I was dating someone they disapproved of.

After an attempt at suicide and weighing only 106 pounds, I was scared, lonely, and hopeless. I cried out to God, hard and long. He met me. My boyfriend at the time gave me a New Testament and told me it was God's Word. "God has words!" I thought. This began my long journey of overcoming depression, suicide, eating disorders, and lack of confidence. Now, 44 years later, I can firmly say that, "He sent His word and healed them and delivered them from their destructions." (Psalm 107:20, KJV) Also, "I shall not die but live and declare the works of the Lord." (Psalm 118:17, KJV) Through the Bible, connecting with the right people, learning the tools that I needed, God took my messes and is making them messages! I praise Him for every storm He has brought me through.

Rosanne Moore, Care Director
www.CRHope.org
CRHope88@gmail.com

Club Med

I mentioned earlier that I used to volunteer at a place where people with life-controlling issues went to find freedom and new life in Christ. The story of how I got there is a long one, but suffice it to say that God sent me to teach there for my own good, and hopefully, the benefit of others. I absolutely loved my time at The Farm and grew a lot as a person and as a minister during that season of my life.

This place was amazing, but it was no Club Med. In other words, it was not like going to a traditional "rehab" like some celebrities go to. These individuals lived on a farm in the middle of nowhere with nothing but cornfields surrounding them. The plumbing and heat didn't always work the best, and they lived in tight quarters. None of that mattered because they had what many traditional rehabs did not have: Jesus.

I want to say that I am not bashing rehabs or any other form of recovery. If that is what it takes to help people, then who am I to speak against it? When I was there, I met individuals who had been to rehab many times. If those forms of treatments had worked for them, however, then they would not have needed to go to The Farm.

Let's face it. When we are talking about any type of recovery or the medical field, there are those who genuinely want to help and others who only want to make money. We cannot lump all forms of treatment into one basket. My belief, however, is that without Jesus, nothing is going to produce fruit that remains.

I really need to explain myself here because I am sure that I will get criticized for being against rehab which is not necessarily true. However, just like anything else, not all rehabs are the same. The word itself is short for rehabilitate which means restore someone to health or normal life by training and therapy after imprisonment, addiction, or illness. I am all for that!

If going to rehab works, then praise God! If Jesus is not involved in the process, however, then it could be a situation where people are going to rehab and only dealing with the symptoms and not the real problem. If I go to the doctor with a sore throat, pain killers will help me feel better. However, if I have an infection, I need an antibiotic to kill it, or I will continue to get worse.

I also want to add that God wastes nothing. Even if going to rehab or something else you've tried didn't help set you free, it was not necessarily a waste of time. Sometimes we need to jump through many hoops before we are ready to surrender to Jesus completely and follow His plan for our lives. Some of us are a little more stubborn than others, and that includes yours truly!

Some rehabs will get people off street drugs and then get them hooked on prescription meds. This may be part of a plan to wean people off gradually, and therefore, a temporary situation. However, if it continues, then it is only a different chain with a new and more socially acceptable name. The person is still stuck, but now the issue is a little more palatable. Let me assure you that Jesus has paid for your complete healing, deliverance, and freedom, and He wants every chain gone! Sometimes it is a gradual process, and that is okay. Whether we are taking baby steps or giant leaps and bounds, we are moving forward on our journey with God.

I am not an expert on every type of addiction or life-controlling issue on the planet. I am not a doctor, scientist, therapist, or counsellor. The only thing that qualifies me to speak on this subject is that I know our Creator who is the ultimate chain breaker, and *He* knows how to set us free from whatever binds us. Sometimes the best we can do is point people to Him and share what He has done for us on our own path to freedom that God tailor-made for us.

One foundational truth that you will probably hear me say a lot is that we are all on a journey. I have come to respect my journey as well as another's. God can use rehab and other tools to get us where He wants us to be. I have known some with addictions who literally walked away and never looked back. I have known others who have broken free only to go back to their vice like a dog returns to its vomit. I don't want to judge what works for anyone, but I also don't want to pretend that people are free from their chains when they are just attached to another one.

Addictions and life-controlling issues are running rampant in our world, and it is time we address this huge problem which is destroying lives daily. We don't need Band-Aids but real answers to tough problems, and God and His wisdom will provide those for us. I do know that His ways are not our ways, and they work! When we leave God out of the equation, however, we can only grasp at straws. We are left to our own devices and have to come up with solutions, programs, and plans with our own smarts which often makes things worse.

There are literally thousands of things people could get addicted to, and I am not going to waste my time researching all of them. What I do want to spend my time and energy on, however, is the One who set the captives free and strive to know Him better. I didn't notice Jesus send a single person to rehab when He walked the earth. Instead He said, "Go and sin no more." As an added bonus, He walks with us on this amazing journey called life. One encounter with Him can literally change everything!

One more time, I am not against rehab if it leads to transformed lives due to relationship with Jesus. However, even if rehab was the magic bullet to put an end to addictions, that is still not going to be an option for many. There are not enough spaces available for every person who needs help. I have seen the price tag of many rehabs, and some people simply cannot afford to go. Others cannot or will not get into these facilities for a variety of reasons. When I taught at The Farm, those it served committed to a one-year program, and although that is admirable, it is not feasible for everyone. That being said, some could argue that The Farm was rehab.

It was a program where people could go to find freedom from the life-controlling issues that had them stuck. Part of that was a time of detox which is obviously necessary in recovery. Most of the program, however, involved learning who God is and who they are in Christ. The Farm provided a place where individuals could renew their minds and develop a relationship with God. As I will discuss later, renewing the mind is critical to victory over our life-controlling issues, and this takes time. At the end of the day, Jesus was the focus, not the chains that had these people bound. Read that again.

One of my favorite scriptures is Jeremiah 29:11 which says, "For I know the plans I have for you," declares the

LORD, "plans to prosper you and not to harm you, plans to give you hope and a future." God has great plans for His children. Those plans are not one-size fits all, but designed specifically for us by our Father. When something is broken, we take it back to the manufacturer for repair. Our Maker is God, and He knows exactly what we need. With Him as our guide, we can all travel different roads and still arrive the same destination, which is freedom in Christ. As long as we follow Him, we'll get there with His perfect plan and impeccable timing.

Voices of Recovery Presents

Joshua

Growing up I was a very happy kid. I was raised in church with a huge family and a place I belonged. My dad worked hard to provide for the family, and my mom stayed home to raise us in a Christian home. I was very poor growing up, but I had joy and happiness. I moved a lot as a young kid, but my family, church, and grandparents were a constant part of my daily life.

At the age of eight we finally got a permanent house. I was homeschooled awhile by my mom, but they decided to put me into public school in the second grade. I was exceedingly smart, but I was not that great at making friends. Kids would make fun of my clothes, my shoes, and even the lunch my mom would pack for me because we could not afford anything else. I really didn't understand why they were using these things against me.

I learned how to get acceptance from people by getting in trouble. I found out very early on that I could make people laugh through sarcasm, quick wit, and using others as the butt of my jokes. This behavior pattern went on, and I had been accepted but labeled into the troublemakers without realizing it.

At 13 years old, I was getting good at making bad choices. I started smoking, drinking, and smoking weed on a regular basis. At 16, I got my license and could go anywhere. My mom would ask me what I was up to, and jokingly I would say that we were going downtown to buy some crack. Laughingly, she would say, "Ok, be safe and save some for me." In reality that's exactly what we were doing and we weren't saving her any.

As my drug use progressed, so did my depression, anxiety, and compulsive behaviors. We had quit going to church a few years prior, and my life was getting pretty messed up. I would work, party, and not come home. I did not notice my mom and dad's marriage was failing and that they started to go drinking and to bars as well since I was not home very often. My parents eventually got a divorce.

I had taught myself how to play guitar and joined a band to further my drug use and started drinking again. Accountability was out the window at my mom's house because she and my new step-dad were never home. Partying had become a way of life, and people were used to meet my needs. My band was doing well as far as the drinking, drugs, and girls went. We got into acid, mushrooms, cocaine, opium, crack, and any other substance we found. I said to myself that at this point I wouldn't live to see 40. I had friends dying around me from living a crazy lifestyle, and I was quickly being consumed completely into a self-destructive way of life.

At the age of 21, I was a recovering alcoholic when I found out I was having a son. Something in me had changed, and I knew I had nine months to get my act together. I got baptized and thought, **This is it, I'm changing my ways.** I quickly got a job at a casino, and the party was now literally all around me.

48

My life was full of money, women, gambling, parties, as well as extreme highs and lows. No way I was ready to stop completely now, so I quit weed and my band, and left my friends. I stayed the same, and so did my lifestyle.

By the time my son was born, I was still an idiot. I tried the best I could to make money, work an honest living, and slow down on the drinking. I took up a career in sheet metal sales and bought a house. My obsessive thinking and compulsive behavior were still very deep-seated, and I was getting very bored of everyday life. I came home and went to work. Life should have been good, but I wanted more excitement.

At 23, I started to mess with something I didn't fully understand. I started selling my wife's prescription of Percocet to a buddy at work. He was giving me an insane amount of money each month for them, and at first, I was thinking, **You're going to give me how much for these?!** What an idiot, this guy is giving me $1,000 for something that costs me eight bucks at the pharmacy.

Naturally, I asked myself why he would do that. So, I decided I would just take two and see what they did. Immediately I realized this is what I had been looking for, a buzz I could get anywhere, that nobody would know about, anytime I wanted, with no side effects. From the first time, I was hooked. Little by little, month after month, I sold less and less and did more and more until eventually I kept them all. I needed them. As my addiction progressed, my moods changed from extreme highs to extreme lows, but I never connected it with the pills. After I found out what withdrawal was, I knew I couldn't go through that again. So instead of stopping my pill use, I went out and found more. I knew I had to be careful and make them last. I couldn't run out or I would get sick and lose my job. I was trapped, so I found my old friends once again and started paying a guy $1000 a month for his prescription. How ironic.

After about two years of that cycle, I was acting off straight emotion and adrenalin. My wife and I were in serious trouble. I blamed her completely for everything. I couldn't understand why she was yelling at me constantly. I tried as hard as I could to hide the fighting from my son. I could see he was being affected big time by our fighting and yelling. He was nervous and was starting to blink uncontrollably and get a few nervous ticks.

Instead of realizing it was all me, I blamed my wife for everything and finally kicked her out. I threatened to take my son to Florida. She was only trying to protect me from myself because I didn't know how to. We got divorced, and I was finally off the leash. I had my house, my son, and the responsibility for taking him to and from school every day and working full-time. Something had to give. I left my job to start my own company, so I could make more money and my own hours. Work was slow, so I began driving from Ohio to Florida every 2 weeks to get pills.

Cops were putting people in jail for up to 30 years if you were caught crossing state lines with drugs, so I would drive 18 hours to Miami, spend 6 hours in line at the doctor's office, and drive 18 hours straight back completely drugged out without sleep. My addiction became immediately worse as I was getting large quantities of drugs on a regular basis, and I was completely dependent. About 6 months after I had started running pills, Florida shut down the pill mills and put an end to it. There was no option but withdrawal.

I went through misery for a month and worked my way out of the control the pills had over me. I had quit pills, but my lifestyle, friends, and habits were the same. Shortly afterwards, I met the love of my life, Kim. Even though I was struggling to stay clean from pills, I wasn't using. We were both divorced and looking to start over with a second chance, but she knew how to party. She didn't do drugs, but we could drink a lot and have a wild lifestyle that consisted of drinking, going to bars and clubs, and such. I finally met someone who could keep up partying and still be a parent and do the home life. As the relationship grew serious, she decided that it was time to make it real, so she backed off the partying. I was definitely not ready or able to stop, and I met the next love of my life: Methadone.

I had finally found my drug of choice. It was a daily progression of getting worse and worse on Methadone. I tried to hide my drug use from my home life to the best of my ability. I didn't bring that lifestyle home and wore multiple masks daily to hide that aspect of my life from my family. Everyone knew something was off, but Kim was in denial. Even if she would bring it up, I lied and tried to make her think she was crazy or yell to the point it wasn't even worth confronting me about it anymore.

Eventually we were married in Mexico in 2010, and I was still struggling with the off and on again use of pills, Methadone, and speed. I was starting to do real damage to my body, mind, family, and marriage as a result of my drug abuse. I was no longer a part of my family even though I was physically there. The grip of Methadone had overtaken me, and I wasn't just using to maintain myself anymore. I was abusing drugs to get higher daily.

I don't really remember a lot of the next 10 years. It was a fog, honestly, with a lot of good times like vacations, birthdays, and Christmas celebrations, but they were heavily outweighed by the bad times like withdrawal, fighting, arguing, and craziness of chasing down pills and getting more. I had severe mood swings and was full of anger most days with any little thing setting me off. My body was broken down, and I was severely malnourished from eating nothing but sugar, drinking Red Bull, and using Methadone and cocaine. My muscles had atrophied from running on fake energy, and my mind was gone. I even had to get most of my teeth replaced.

During this time, I lived in a complete state of fear and isolation outside of my drug buddies. I tried to control everyone in my family as a reflection of that fear. It was only a matter of time before something happened. One day, coming home from work, I walked in to find my wife had moved out. I did not even notice the damage I was doing to everyone around me. My son was heartbroken to lose her and scared to be alone with me. I was off the leash again, and this time I went full steam ahead. I was using more than ever, and depression really set in.

My wife and I were living apart, and I started selling cocaine and Methadone to get by. I was using more than I was selling. I eventually had plenty of cash and enough drugs stashed away to not have to worry about running out. I finally had everything I wanted yet realized I had nothing to live for. My family was gone; my friends were hollow, and I was dead inside. I was trapped in a lifestyle of my own making, and my mind was a complete wasteland. In a pit of despair I just couldn't do enough drugs to cover up my feelings and emotions or get high enough anymore to not notice what was going on around me. I felt myself falling apart from the inside, and nothing I could use or do could help me. I was in a very dark place.

I have no clue what was going on in my mind at the time. Besides that, I was trapped, and there was only one way out at this point. On September 18, 2018, I asked myself if it could be the drugs. No! It was everyone else, and I was obviously deep in denial. I put a gun to my head and pulled the trigger. Immediately, I regretted it. Today, I thank the Lord the bullet got jammed in the chamber. I quickly fell to my knees and cried out to Jesus to save me, and I was rescued from my life like one escaping from a fire.

I had not known my dad very well, but I ended up at

his house in tears, broken down by life and asked him if my
son and I could stay with him awhile. He said I could, and I was
clinging to the only thing that I knew was stable, and that was
Jesus. I was deathly sick coming off not only Methadone, but
also cocaine, Adderall, and methamphetamines. The following
week, my uncle Dave, who was in AA at the time, invited me to a
meeting where I got my first 24-hour day of sobriety. The next 18
days I slept a total of 22 hours and attended 18 meetings, sick as
a dog. I was praying constantly, reaching out to members of AA
and NA to keep from using, and starting to grow stronger in my
relationship with Jesus while also attending church. I was keeping Kim posted about how many days I had stayed clean, but she
had heard it all before, and even though she didn't want to hear
it again, she was listening.

I was being made new and was walking a new path
that I had never walked down before. Unfortunately, I had to
walk down it without my wife. It was just me and God for the
next three months. I was led to Celebrate Recovery* in my third
month of sobriety and finally felt like I was home. I had found
that feeling I had been longing for since I was a child. God was
restoring my life, only this time the way He wanted me to live it,
using Celebrate Recovery and each and every person I encoun-
tered as a tool to teach me how to live a life worth living. Sticking
to the eight principals and the 12 steps, I was being taught how
to live one day at a time and enjoy one moment at a time. I was
being completely remade from the inside out.

I realized God gave me the power to decide to stay sober

and make positive changes or to go back down a road I knew all too well. The days have added up quickly, and I had found I was living a new life I could be proud of. I found self-worth, acceptance, love, compassion, and joy while having a good time sober, and surrounded by hope. My thoughts were transformed into thinking positively and being grateful for everything including just being alive, and living the abundant life Jesus promised.

As I continued my journey, others were attracted to my new found grace and way of life, including my wife. She never had a chance, haha! The changes that were being made within me were undeniable. Jesus was working and moving in every part of my recovery and life just because I surrendered to His will for me. My dad started going to church with me, and my sisters started coming to Celebrate Recovery to find out how to get what I had. My family was leaning on me as a supporter instead of the one needing the support. My son was getting close to me and even starting to laugh again.

About 6 months into recovery I joined my first closed group. I had to dig deeper and find the roots of my obsessive and compulsive behaviors and find what my triggers were so I could watch for them. I learned how to trust other people, and how to open my past to heal and learn from it instead of not looking at it and carrying it around every day with me. Now, I had been putting prayers up on the prayer cross for months that my wife would come back. After so long in my new life, I realized just coming back wasn't enough, so I put a new prayer on the cross that Kim would find Jesus and then come back.

Kim was saved and gave her life to Jesus. I saw changes happen in her heart, and later that month she was baptized, and we were back together in church. In a little over 12 months of living a new way, I have graduated my closed group, realized it is possible to make positive changes, and have seen total restoration take place throughout my entire life. Don't get me wrong; I went through a lot of pain and hardships along the way, but I stayed focused on doing the next right thing and surrendering my will daily.

I now have a brand new life that I wouldn't give up for anything, a church I can call my home, a recovery group I look forward to seeing daily, great friends, and a marriage that's based on good values. I couldn't have made it this far without the support of others, and of course Jesus, who changed everything for me.

I want to end with a short prayer. Father, I thank You for not allowing the lowest points of my life to limit my potential. Thank You for giving a divine purpose to someone as imperfect as me. I praise You for Your amazing power that carries us in moments of weakness, and I know You will lead each one of us where You want us to be. Thank You, Jesus, for showing us that incredible things start from humble beginnings, and through Your mercy, each one of us can have a life worth living if we turn to You. It's in Your name I pray. Amen.

Joshua B.
*Celebrate Recovery: www.CelebrateRecovery.com

Ding, Dong, the Witch is Dead!

When I would talk about traditional rehab with the people at The Farm, I would tell them my idea to start my own rehab. I could guarantee that 100% of those who walked through my doors would never use again. They looked at me in disbelief wondering how that would even be possible.

It's really quite simple. When clients entered my rehab, I would kill them. See, they will never use again. Of course, I am not serious. My facility would not be open very long, and I would quickly find myself in jail for my horrific methods. Kind? No. Effective? Yes! (Again, I am not serious, so if you work in law enforcement, there is no need to come knocking on my door!)

I have often heard people talk about their loved ones who are facing addiction. They say that it is like there are two separate people, the addict, and the relative. Families have to set boundaries and deal with the addict while still trying to love, support, and help their loved one. This is a tricky tightrope to walk, and my heart breaks for people who have children gripped by addictions or life-controlling issues.

What if the addict could be killed, and the loved one could remain? This seems impossible in the natural, but God has provided the answer for each and every one of us who struggle with some type of unwanted habit or addiction. The answer is the cross!

One of the most powerful Scriptures that you will ever read is Galatians 2:20. I love The Passion Translation which says, "My old identity has been co-crucified with Messiah and no longer lives; *for the nails of his cross crucified me with Him.* And now the essence of this new life is no longer mine, for the Anointed One lives His life through me—*we live in union as one*! My new life is empowered by the faith of the Son of God who loves me so much that He gave Himself for me and dispenses His life into mine!"

If you have come to faith in Christ, then you, too, have been crucified with Him. Say, what? Yep, the old you is deader than a hammer. The new you is alive and well. As the title of the chapter says, "Ding, Dong, the Witch is Dead!"

If you are a Christian, then maybe you have been baptized. I am not talking about getting sprinkled as a baby. I am talking about getting immersed into water to declare publicly that you are a follower of Jesus. Getting dunked in water symbolizes the death of the old you. Coming up out of the water represents you coming to new life in Christ. We have made these things religious and ceremonial instead of recognizing the profound meaning our rebirth has for our lives!

If we could grasp this reality, then it would solve the issues, addictions, and habits that we face. Maybe you have tried rehab like many of the individuals at The Farm. The reason that many of these places don't have a high success rate is simple. They are trying to "fix" the old you. Have you ever tried to clean up or improve someone who is not fixable? It doesn't work at all, but we still try to accomplish this feat, which only leaves us defeated and exhausted.

This truth is so simple that it's hard to wrap our minds around it. You may not be able to see it because most people look at everything with their natural eyes. You look in the mirror and the "old you" seems alive and well, but spiritually speaking, the old you is no longer alive if you have gone to the cross. Most individuals spend almost all of their time and energy trying to solve a problem that was solved over two thousand years ago! Here is an amazing truth that really sums up everything I will discuss in this book: *Jesus didn't just die for you; He died **as** you.* Read that again.

The bottom line is this: Jesus didn't come to fix you; He came to crucify you and start over. The good (no, great) news is that you don't have to crawl up on the cross to get this done. Because of His amazing love, He did it for you and as you. Believers were spiritually crucified with Him, and now they can enjoy the freedom and joy that comes with discovering who they really are in Him. Welcome to the new you!

I cannot emphasize the power of the cross enough. Religion says that we have to earn something, follow rules, or basically try to work our way up to God. Christianity says that God came to us in the form of His Son, Jesus. Can you imagine the pain, suffering, and humiliation that Jesus went through on the cross? He even asked the Father if there was another way not once, not twice, but three times in the Garden of Gethsemane. I didn't see where God provided a "plan B."

God has provided a solution for each and every problem mankind faces. Why don't we all simply receive it? Hosea 4:6 has the answer. It says that God's people are destroyed because of a lack of knowledge. What don't we know? That we are loved. That we are free. That we are safe. That He is Lord. That He has provided a way out of our mess. That He saves. That we belong in a family as His beloved children. That He came to give us new life in Him. We must recognize that we have an enemy who is bound and determined to keep us in the dark when it comes to the freedom in the Light. Ignorance is NOT bliss!

The cross is the answer to the struggles we face. Because of His amazing love, Jesus went to the cross for you and *as you.* If you have received this gift of grace, then the old you that you have been trying to fix, improve, and rehabilitate exists no more. The old you is DEAD, so stop trying to fix him/her. Now walk in the new life that Jesus's resurrection has provided for you. I will explain more on this later because it is critical in moving forward!

Voices of Recovery Presents
Someone's Mom

As of September, 2019, my son has been in recovery from heroin addiction for five years. He is currently 27 years old. My story of his road to recovery is just that, my story and not his. I often ask myself why he has survived, and others haven't. I have survivor's guilt, but share my story hoping it will be a voice of hope. There are many people who do recover from addiction. People experience recovery in various ways: 12 step programs, medical assistance, psychological therapy, faith-based programs, and other ways. My son had access to all of these tools in his attempt to get clean. My husband and I were fortunate because our son was mostly willing to try these resources...to try to get better. He didn't want to be an addict. During the course of his addiction, he became transformed by faith in God. I believe this transformation is a significant reason he achieved recovery and has sustained it.

In retrospect, many of the things I witnessed in my son's recovery could be seen, by some, as divine intervention and to others, as simple coincidences. His second rehab experience was in a 30-day in-patient facility. One sunny, spring day after visiting my son in rehab, I was sitting at the table on my deck. I was tearfully praying for him. I desperately wanted to know if God could hear my prayers. I wasn't asking for him to be healed but rather asking for an acknowledgement of my prayers. In that very moment, a small bird landed on the table in front of me, then a second bird, and then a third bird-all chickadees. Each bird was so close I could have touched them without reaching out. I was frozen with what I was witnessing. Each bird cocked its head and looked at me and then flew away. Was it just a coincidence or was it a sign that my prayers were being heard? I have accepted the latter. God or some greater power was listening, and I knew there was hope for my son.

After attempting two tries at rehab, my son's addiction was getting worse. On a whim I bought plane tickets for my son and his sister to visit their older sister in Omaha for a long weekend. My husband and I naively thought maybe this little trip would give him a chance to be separated from the things pulling him toward heroin at home. The morning they were to leave for the airport, he overdosed in our home. We found him in the shower passed out, lips blue and skin grey, but alive. Within minutes he was awake and standing up.... insisting he was still going to get on the plane to go see his sister. We drove him to the airport that morning in time to catch his flight. I was frantic that we had made the wrong decision but knew this disease of addiction had taken over every part of our son. While he was with his sisters, my husband and I spent the weekend on the phone searching for help, searching for another rehab location. We were willing to do anything to save him. We found a place in California that would take him, and with the encouragement of his sisters, he left Omaha and flew to California for his third attempt at rehab. Was it a coincidence or divine intervention in the way things played out that particular weekend? He survived a near deadly overdose, and this crazy pre-planned trip brought him together with his supportive sisters and halfway to the location of his third attempt at rehab. While driving in the car after being picked up at the Los Angeles airport by the rehab staff, he called me and said, "Mom, I am on the Santa Monica freeway, and I am going to be ok." Later that day I found out that this was the feast day of Saint Monica. Saint Monica was known for her prayerful life dedicated to her wayward son, Augustine.

My son spent nearly nine months in California in rehab. When he returned home, he announced he had connected through Facebook with a girl from his high school. They began dating, and he began relapsing again. Addiction recovery for my son was always two steps forward and one step back. Relapse, of course, is part of recovery. This young woman came from a family whose faith in the Catholic Church was the center of their lives. What are the chances of my son beginning a relationship with someone of such great faith...coincidence or divine intervention? We raised our children in the Episcopal Church, so going to church was nothing new to my son. However, since his late high school years, attending church was not a priority. Attending mass not only on Sunday, but also on the required holy days, was a priority for his girlfriend. Unlike my son, she had never used drugs and rarely drank alcohol. She was aware of his heroin addiction, and her family quickly became aware of it also. There were many months of ugliness addiction brought to all of our lives. My husband and I, as well as his girlfriend's parents, would beg her to leave him. She refused to give up on him. One evening, he announced he was going to go through the process necessary to be baptized in the Catholic Church. I remember this moment clearly. He was sitting on the couch with his coat still on. He said he needed to be forgiven, and that the church will give him this forgiveness. He seemed so confident and relieved to have made this choice. My son felt a lot of guilt and shame about his addiction. For the next 6 months he juggled a few college classes, his religious education classes, and worked part-time. He stayed clean for most of this time and was baptized into the Catholic Church. I was witnessing a transformation in my son's life.

My son had learned a lot about managing heroin addiction, but once again he relapsed. His faith and baptism still were not enough to keep him clean. He went back to a 30-day in-patient rehab. He spoke to his girlfriend very little during these 30 days, and I was sure that this would be the end of their relationship. I was wrong, and after the 30 days were over, their relationship continued. Her mother told me she could no longer try to convince her daughter to end the relationship with my son. She said the only thing she could do now was to pray for him daily. Once again, I felt that something greater was being revealed. How could I give up hope on my son, when this woman was so willing to hold on to hope? My son attended Narcotics Anonymous meetings daily, and church remained a priority. Going to confession and church became a type of therapy for him. After he participated in these things, he would come home looking like a new person. I could see the physical changes in him.

Since his last in-patient rehab in 2014, he has maintained his sobriety, graduated from college, found employment, married his girlfriend, had a son, and is now expecting a daughter. They continue to make their faith the center of their lives. The journey to recovery for my son and for the people in his life was also filled with dark days and many struggles. He made use of many tools available to get clean: suboxone, vivitrol, psychological services, in-and out-patient rehab, Narcotics Anonymous meetings, and cutting all ties with people in his life who were not helpful with his sobriety. I believe all these resources helped him achieve recovery. However, I also witnessed the development of my son's faith and believe this transformation was a significant factor in his recovery. I am profoundly saddened by the loss so many have experienced as a result of addiction. I share my story because I want others to have hope and to know that many people do recover.

Hypnotized and Traumatized

Our mind is powerful, but it can easily be deceived. Imagine that you go to a hypnotist, and you volunteer to get up on stage. This entertainer convinces you that you are a dog. You suddenly get down on all fours and start barking at the audience who erupts in laughter and cheers. The moment you lift your leg on the podium brings the house down. Everyone thinks it's funny except your spouse. I mean, you are really embarrassing yourself, and the videos of you are going viral and getting tons of likes and comments.

The hypnotist sends you back to your seat, but in your mind, you are a dog. You don't know what to do. Your spouse then comes to guide you back to your spot (and you are wagging your imaginary tail for all it's worth). After the show, your spouse tries to find the hypnotist, but he is long gone. It is time to go home and let your kids know that Mom/Dad is gone, but they now have a new puppy to love!

What to do now? Try to get you to stand up? Convince you to stop eating out of the dog dish? Get you to use the toilet instead of lifting your leg on the couch? Try to keep you from fighting with the cat? You really need some *rehabilitation*, but this is all going to be very laborious work that could take years! We may even need to find a specialized rehab that deals with people who think they are dogs. The process is going to be very expensive, and of course, humans who think they are dogs cannot go to work. By the way, this year's family Christmas gathering is going to be pretty awkward!

Okay, I hope you get my point. The key to fixing people who think they are dogs is not to put them through rigorous behavior modification rituals. It is not to send them to dog obedience school. Only one thing is needed: Let them know that they are humans **not** dogs. *In other words, the behaviors will change once the mindset changes.* Read that again.

Let me ask you this question. What is wrong with someone who believes he/she is a dog? Absolutely nothing! The problem is simple. The person believes a lie. How do you solve this problem? You counter the lie with the truth. Some will receive it instantly, and others will take a while, but eventually it will sink in. Then and only then, will behavior change.

I wish it were that easy to tell people with an addiction or life-controlling issue that there is nothing wrong with them, and that they are just believing lies. Their deception keeps them stuck until the lightbulb comes on and hopefully realize that their freedom is available. We can present people with the truth, but it usually takes God lighting it up for them to see it.

I remember hearing about how elephants become broken so that they can be used in a circus and other entertainment venues. A young elephant is tied with ropes and beaten into submission until its spirit is literally broken. After this cruel process is complete, the elephant can be held down by a tiny rope. We all know that the elephant can easily snap the rope and run off to freedom. However, it is so mentally crushed that it won't even try.

Just like the "dog" in the previous example, this majestic creature believes a lie. What is the lie? That it cannot break free from whatever has it bound because it is not strong enough to do so. Are humans any different? We can easily break the chains that bind us with God's strength residing on the inside of us. However, if we don't know what He has done on our behalf, we stay bound by tiny chains that could be snapped in an instant! The same power that raised Jesus from the dead lives in us as believers. (Romans 8:11) That resurrection power does us no good if we are ignorant of it or refuse to access it!

Let's take a brief history lesson to highlight this point. In 1863, President Abraham Lincoln signed a document called the Emancipation Proclamation. It declared that all slaves were to be freed. Do you know how many slaves entered into freedom because of this document? The answer is zero. Why? Because they were kept in darkness about the legal action that provided their freedom. In other words, they believed a lie, too.

Masters were not in a big rush to let their slaves know that freedom had been provided. Of course, they wanted to keep their "property" from knowing that they had been given the right to leave the plantation. The slaves were legally free, but because the truth was kept from them, they stayed bound in slavery. The enemy, the one who keeps people enslaved, deceives people which keeps them in bondage. Once people realize the truth, however, they can act on it.

John 8:32 says that it is the *knowledge* of the truth that sets us free. This is not head knowledge but experiential "knowing" or intimacy with our Savior. Our "Emancipation Proclamation" was signed over two thousand years ago by Jesus. His death, burial, and resurrection provided freedom from bondage and salvation for every person on the planet. Obviously, not everyone has taken advantage of this amazing gift. A gift must be received for it to be effective. Once we know or experience what Jesus has done, then the truth of what He did can benefit us. We are no longer slaves with a wicked taskmaster but sons and daughters of the Most High God!

Again, we need to renew our minds to these truths. God has provided this free gift of salvation that we could, never in a million years, earn. Instead of receiving the gift, however, many are trying to earn what has already been given. Some feel like they must fix themselves, *then* come to Jesus. This puts us on a treadmill going nowhere. Without accessing what He did on the cross, we'll never get better!

Speaking of treadmills, many are trying to behavior mod themselves into improving. That is like trying to change the actions of a person who thinks he/she is a dog. It might work for a bit, then the old habits creep back in. Why? Because the mind hasn't been renewed. True change, or should I say transformation, comes from the inside out.

First, we realize who we are in our minds and hearts, and then we will notice our behaviors will line up with these truths. As soon as the person figures out that he/she is not a dog, the barking will stop along with chasing the cat and chewing up shoes! The person was born a human, but believing a lie about himself/herself will keep the deception going until revelation comes.

A key Scripture to illustrate the importance of mind renewal is this: "Do not conform to the pattern of this world, but be transformed by the renewing of your mind. Then you will be able to test and approve what God's will is—His good, pleasing and perfect will." (Romans 12:2)

We have established that for Christians, Jesus took the old self and crucified him/her on the cross. That was finished over two thousand years ago. The only thing to do is believe it and receive it by faith. I wish it was as easy as flipping a switch, but mind renewal can take a long time. The more we are in the Word and meditating on what God says about us, the faster it will come.

God's Word will transform from the inside out. I remember when I first came to Jesus, I bought myself a Bible and began reading it daily. I didn't understand it at first, but over time I could not ignore the fact that Jesus loved me and came to set me free, not only from the things that had me bound, but also the consequences of my past mistakes. I started to see myself, not as an unloved "orphan," but as a beloved child of God. This was like a cup of cool water as I wandered around the desert.

I am guessing that a lot of your issues are the result of a faulty mindset. You may think you're a "dog," but you really are a son/daughter of the Most High God. It's time to stop barking! You are royalty, and once you realize that, your actions will follow. You may be like that beaten-down elephant who is "bound" by something so tiny that you believe the lie that you cannot break free. Like the mighty elephant, I pray you will snap that rope and move forward into your freedom. It's time to roar!

Voices of Recovery Presents

Dave

I recently spoke on a live video broadcast across a popular social media platform, and I talked openly about my long battle with a pornography addiction that nearly destroyed my marriage. It was the first time I revealed this part of my life in such a large public setting. My sister saw the video and was in shock. She immediately called me, and among other things, wanted to know why she never knew about this. How could so many years have gone by, and she never knew the pain and suffering my wife and I had experienced? The answer was simple: people spend just as much time and energy concealing their addictions from the outside world as they do feeding the monster that lives secretly inside them. Both of those two priorities, fueling the monster and hiding its existence, consume the addict and keep them in a perpetual cycle driven by the unholy trinity of shame, fear, and control.

While every addict's journey to his or her personal dark pit of hell is unique, there are some general commonalities that hold true across the board. My story, while very personal and exclusive to me, shares some of these common threads. A history of sexual sin in my family line introduced a generational component into the equation. Some level of childhood trauma left me with unresolved heart wounds, and as a teenager and young adult I learned to self-medicate through fantasy and masturbation.

In my mid-twenties I entered into a very unhealthy marriage that did nothing but deepen the preexisting heart wounds and intensify my quest to ease the pain. The protracted and contested divorce that followed 10 years later left me completely broken as I watched the suffering that our children endured. I came out of that experience totally exposed and vulnerable against the enemy's attempt to take me out with a sex and pornography addiction—it was the only thing at my disposal to ease the pain. Of course, the thing that left me completely defenseless to this onslaught was the fact that I had walked away from the Lord.

This was the baggage I brought into my second marriage, and it didn't take long for my addiction to be exposed. The early years of my second marriage wound up being just as unhealthy as my first, but the beginning of the turnaround came when we got back into church, and my wife got serious about pursuing her own inner healing. For the first time in my life, I made a concerted effort to find freedom from my addiction, but no matter how hard I tried, I couldn't break the chains through my own power. Because I was still broken and wounded, I remained trapped in the fear, shame, and control cycle which drove me to conceal the truth at all costs. I learned how to become a very accomplished liar, and there was no level too low to stoop to in order to conceal the monster that remained inside me. The breaking point for me came when it became evident that our marriage was on the verge of failure. My wife was ready to walk out. Every bone in her body wanted to run; she was done. The only thing that kept her from leaving me was her desire to be obedient and faithful to the Lord.

When you reach your breaking point, you realize two things. You can't do it alone, and you have to shine a light into the deepest, darkest places in your soul. My journey to freedom wasn't instantaneous; it was a hard-fought process over many years. I went through a number of inner healing sessions, broke off generational curses, and started to pursue a much more personal and intimate relationship with the Lord. During this time, I made real progress, but there were also some setbacks as I hadn't yet dug deep enough to get to the root. The final stage in my healing journey came with the completion of an intensive, five-day inner healing program, followed by a 10-week group study with other men coming out of pornography addiction. These were the last and the biggest steps that finally secured my victory.

I'm happy to say that my marriage has been completely restored and is thriving with new and ever-deepening levels of love and intimacy. My wife and I are involved in several outreach ministries, and we have even started our own marriage mentoring program. God has truly blessed us by turning our mess into our message, a message of hope, redemption, and resurrection. We believe it's never too late for anyone, and that all things are possible in Christ. I bless you in your journey toward healing and freedom, and I celebrate with you in anticipation of your victory over addiction.

Dave McCrery
www.MarriageOutoftheBox.com

Voices of Recovery Presents

Kirsten

I never dreamed this story would be mine.

Over 13 years ago, my world shattered. My husband of 25 years revealed his pornography addiction. Shocked, wounded to the core, I listened as he poured out the addiction that threatened his job, our marriage and family, and life.

Until that moment, I believed we had a decent marriage. Yes, we struggled like most couples do, but our relationship seemed solid. But, with this revelation, everything changed. Hurt, betrayed, wounded to the core, I didn't trust my husband any longer, nor was I sure I knew him.

However, one thread of hope kept me going—we heard it didn't have to be fatal. God works miracles even when you aren't looking for them. We immediately reached out to friends who provided hope and a lifeline to healing when we couldn't think, breathe, or process the next step.

And that's what we needed to hear. Within 24 hours we had a recovery plan formulated. My husband arranged to meet with a counselor and decided on the next step. Over the next 18 months, we sought intensive marriage counseling and regular support from a spiritual restoration team. God made Himself evident each step of the process.

Some lessons learned:

· Isolation creates danger. Without realizing it, we did not have a strong network of friends. Identifying 4-6 people to form our spiritual care team proved a challenge, which alerted us to the dangerous position we'd allowed ourselves to get into. Satan loves to isolate us and foster the lie that we can manage life alone. When we believe that lie, we become easy prey to Satan's schemes.

· Truth triumphs. Satan insinuates that telling the truth brings danger and rejection. But God's Word says that the truth sets us free. (John 8:32) And that's exactly our experience. From the first people we told, each person assured us of their love and respect for us. Yes, this addiction could not remain, but recovery would happen.

· Authentic relationships nurture. Today, more than 13 years later, our marriage looks totally different. God didn't give me back my marriage; He remade it. He restores the broken-hearted and heals the wounded soul.

God IS able to bring beauty out of the destruction we make of our lives.

Kirsten D. Samuel
KirstenDSamuel.com

Editor's Note: Dave and Kirsten are not married to each other, but they share about the same issue from different perspectives, so we put their testimonies together.

Big Buts

I wish that we were sitting in a cozy café and drinking a cup of coffee right now. I would love to look you in the eye and discuss these truths. When the light bulb comes on, and God brings the revelation, there is nothing like it!

I can hear people saying, "Yeah, but you don't know what I have done. Yeah, but you can't expect me to believe it's that easy. Yeah, but I've tried this Jesus thing, and it didn't work." Wow, those are some big buts!

Well, I have a bigger (ahem) but for you: BUT GOD! He knows what you have done and loves you anyway. While we were stuck in our sin and dysfunction, Christ died for us. (Romans 5:8) Many people mistakenly believe that they must get their lives in order before coming to God. Nothing could be further from the truth! That is like saying that as soon as you get over your illness, you can go see your doctor. Without Jesus, nothing is going to get fixed, anyway!

One common response to the grace of God is that people think that they are too far gone for God to love and help them. This is especially true of Christians who have had continual struggles and setbacks. They think that God is so fed up and disgusted that He has given up on them. I want to reassure those with similar thoughts that they're not that powerful!

One of my favorite stories in the Bible is in the Book of Hosea. God told the Prophet Hosea to marry a prostitute. We can skim over this quickly, but imagine what would happen if God gave these instructions to your pastor, and he went to where women are selling their bodies for money to find his future bride. That would be scandalous and might make the "prayer chain" pretty quickly!

Hosea obeyed God even when it didn't make sense and married Gomer. She began to bring forth children, but they were not Hosea's. That's right; she was cheating on him. What did God tell the prophet to do? He said to go and get his wife and bring her home. Say what? Hosea had a legal right to divorce his wife, but instead, he continued to stay committed and faithful to her. Gomer even got sold into slavery, and God told Hosea to buy her back. Wow!

This story rings a bell with me because I was once an unfaithful wife who did something similar. Yes, this is a big part of my story and the "boulder" I referred to earlier. When I first read this book in the Bible, I cried an ugly cry because I could clearly see God's love for me despite my mistakes. Jesus is showing His "unfaithful bride" the lengths that He will go to in order to bring her back into the loving arms of the Father. This is unconditional love like no other.

Gomer continued to wander, but she eventually realized how much she was loved by her husband. Hosea could have divorced her or left her in slavery, but he didn't. He went into the wilderness to find his bride and bring her home! This, my friend, is a beautiful picture of God's love for us. He will continue to love and rescue us until we finally get it and come home. He is crazy about us, and nothing we can do will separate us from His infinite love!

I did a study on the meaning of Gomer's name. Can you guess what it means? Slut? Whore? Tramp? Adulterer? Fornicator? Floozy? Those names represent her actions, but her given name means "complete." We are complete in Christ, and our actions (good or bad) don't change that fact. However, how many of us are living in this truth? The enemy's deception is that we lack something. The serpent used lack to deceive Adam and Eve in the original Garden of Eden. They, too, were complete with absolutely everything they needed, including God's presence, but Satan convinced them that they lacked something, and that opened the door to them sinning.

One common argument to the unconditional love and grace of God is this: *So, if God loves us no matter what, should we just keep on sinning?* As the Apostle Paul said, "By no means!" (I would read Romans 6 to get further insight on this truth.) Once the bride understands that she lacks nothing, she will stop straying as she recognizes that her needs are met by one person alone, her husband. You probably know that we, as believers, are the Bride of Christ, and He is our eternal Bridegroom. What a great picture of His amazing love for us!

We don't really deserve this kind of love, but God lavishes it on us anyway because He is Love. Here is a "big but" that will help us understand it: *You see, at just the right time, when we were still powerless, Christ died for the ungodly. Very rarely will anyone die for a righteous person, though for a good person someone might possibly dare to die.* **But God** *demonstrates his own love for us in this: While we were still sinners, Christ died for us.* (Romans 5:6-8)

No more "Yeah, buts." He loves you. Just like Gomer, when you realize it, you, too, will stop straying and come home.

Voices of Recovery Presents

"L"

I grew up in the projects with my mom and brothers. I looked around and knew I was different. I didn't look like anyone else in my own family. There was no man in our home. I saw other kids with dads and wondered where mine was. I would ask my mom, and she would change the subject. As I got older, I kept asking. Nothing.

I figured my dad must be a pretty important man. When I walked around the streets, I looked at men and wondered, "Is that him? Is that my dad?" They didn't look like me, but I wondered. Maybe he's the mayor. Maybe he's a police officer. He could be someone famous on TV. Maybe he's looking for me.

I had to know. One day I was with my mom, and I would not let up. "Who is my daddy? You have to tell me." I kept on and could see she was getting mad.

Finally she slammed her hand down on the table and screamed, "I don't know! Whoever put the money on the table that night is your dad. You happy now?"

Something inside died that day. The hurt was too much, and I got angry. Angry with my mom, angry with a man I'd never know, angry with the world. Just angry and nowhere to go with it. My dad was no one important. He was not coming to rescue me. He probably didn't even know I existed. I think what died in me that day was hope.

I roamed the streets which is dangerous for a girl in the hood. I joined a gang, and there I found the love and acceptance I never got from my family. They had my back, and I had theirs. I belonged. I did what it took to gain their respect. When I walked the streets of the city, I carried a gun at all times. I felt powerful. I felt important. I felt loved and respected.

One thing led to another, and I started to get in trouble. I got arrested many times for dealing, stealing, and such. I didn't care. Like I said, I was dead inside, and nothing fazed me. My thought was, **Lock me up and throw away the key. It don't matter to me.**

I did something then, and was looking at a long prison sentence. That was one thing I didn't want. My lawyer said that I could avoid jail time if I went to a place. What place? Well, it was through a church, and if I completed the program, I may get a reduced sentence or not have to go to prison at all.

Church? Seriously, I wanted no part of that, but I also did not want to go to prison. I said I would go. It was another world. I had to take classes and started to learn things I missed out on when I dropped out of school. That was good but I didn't like the women there who did not respect me or understand just who I was. When I was in the city, I was a big deal. Now I had to live with them and try to get along or get sent to prison.

They talked about Jesus all the time. This really got on my nerves. I tried to keep my mouth shut, but you know, it was not easy for me. I almost got kicked out a couple times for disrespecting people. I was not used to giving respect but getting it. I knew how to get it where I came from, but this place wasn't like that.

I wanted to bust out of there like nobody's business. I thought about it many times, but, being out in the middle of nowhere, I was not in my element. I told myself to get through it, stay in your lane, then you can get back to the city and back to real life.

Yeah, that was the plan. One day in worship, they played a song about a good Father. The words father and dad just got me going. I hated those words. I put up walls. Those words brought back memories of my mom's fist slamming on the table and telling me things I did not want to hear.

God don't play. He knows how to tear down walls. Brick by brick He started pulling them down. I tried to build them back up again, but I was getting tired; so very tired. He would take the bricks out of my hand and put them on the ground. He got me. During morning worship one day, I just went up to the wooden cross in the front of the chapel and fell on my knees. I cried for the first time since I was a little girl. I mean, the tears would not stop. Women surrounded me. Women I had cursed and even wanted to kill. They loved on me. They saw me. God saw me. He knew.

I graduated from the program and went back to the city. I knew in five minutes I could not live there anymore. I moved to a quiet place and keep to myself a lot. I pray for my kids, for my family. God is healing me. I can't go back to the old ways. I am learning to live in the 'new' one day at a time. The father I looked for my whole life was right there all the time. He wanted me. He wanted ME. I was born to be Papa's girl. That's all I need.

Hamster Wheels

Have you ever watched a hamster on a wheel? That little guy is running like the dickens, and he is going nowhere. Yes, he is working hard, but he is still in the same place. Sound familiar?

I, too, have been on the hamster wheel, and it is not fun. The harder you work, the faster you go, and the more exhausted you become. However, you have not advanced one bit. Eventually you give up and quit trying. Again, sound familiar?

Maybe part of your wheel experience has been going to rehab. I don't want to beat a dead horse, but if that is what God is using to bring freedom to your life, who am I to criticize that? God wastes nothing, so don't berate yourself about the things that didn't work so well for you, whatever they may be. When we get into desperate situations, we will do anything to make the cycles of pain and dysfunction stop.

So you go to rehab (or something else) and try to fix the old you. It works for a while, but you begin to give into temptation. The people who supported (or even paid for) you to go into some program are frustrated with you. You're mad at yourself and want to be further along in recovery than you are. Relationships are strained or completely broken. You feel so bad about yourself that the only thing that brings relief is the very thing that got you stuck in the first place. (Hamster wheel up; hamster wheel down.)

Sometimes frustration is a good thing. It lets us know that we are not satisfied with the status quo, so we take different steps to move forward. The good news is that Jesus took that action for us by going to the cross as us. The key to accessing it is to believe and receive it. Things may still look the same on the outside, but eventually they will line up with what is happening on the inside. Instead of trying to "fix" the old you, receive the fact that this person was crucified, dead, and buried with Jesus. Jump off the hamster wheel and start walking with Him!

What happened to our Savior after three days in the tomb? That's right, He was raised to new life again. Here is a mind-blowing truth: *The same power that raised Jesus from the dead lives in His followers.* (Romans 8:11) I could meditate on that Scripture for years and not grasp its fullness. Resurrection life resides in us, yet are we taking full advantage of this dynamic power?

Because of Jesus, we have access to this gift of new life. What does it take? Faith! God provided a way out of our messes. He took on our guilt, shame, issues, habits, hang-ups, addictions, etc. and gave us a brand-new life in Him. Now that is not just good news, it is great news!

If you are on the hamster wheel, I urge you to get off. Stop trying to put lipstick on a corpse and recognize that the old you is dead and gone. The truth of the matter is that the old you is not even fixable. No offense, but it is the truth. The old me wasn't fixable either! I had to go to the cross and let her be crucified. This is *the key* to victorious living in Christ. It is God's ultimate solution, but it can take us a bit to raise the white flag of surrender and receive this amazing gift.

The old you is not fixable, but crucifiable. Thankfully you don't have to get on the cross yourself. The great exchange is that someone did that on your behalf because of His great love for <u>you</u>. One of my all-time favorite verses is this: *Therefore, if anyone is in Christ, the new creation has come: The old has gone, the new is here!* (2 Corinthians 5:17)

Sometimes we need to go through a lot of running on hamster wheels before we can receive this amazing truth. Some of us are a little more hard-headed than the rest, but God will let you run until you get sick and tired of being sick and tired. Once you get off, you can start moving forward with the Holy Spirit. He is compared to fire, wind, and a river. You know what those three things have in common? They are powerful, and they MOVE forward and not just around in circles!

Like many people, we look to the world to solve our problems. The world has been blinded to the truth of God's love, power, and ability to help us out of our messes. If we don't know Jesus, how can we expect Him to fix things for us? Don't be too hard on yourself. Now that you know the truth (or are being exposed to it), you can begin to do things His way. It's a new day!

God has done His part by sending Jesus to die in your place. He is waiting for you to surrender, trust Him, and receive His forgiveness and new life. It is a process and a journey, and it is not always easy. You know what else is not easy? Staying stuck on a hamster wheel going nowhere fast. Once you get off, you can begin to move forward. One of God's most amazing creatures can shed more light on this truth.

Voices of Recovery Presents

Francine

Happy, sad, glad, or mad, I fed my emotions. "Comfort foods" became my emotional crutch for coping. It was my "go to" for everything. Unfortunately, overeating only temporarily relieved my emotional pain and instead left me worse off and more frustrated than before. I was always physically feeling bad, and I continually struggled with weight gain. Most of my emotional eating happened in secret, going out at night for ice cream, keeping junk food in my desk, and always eating in my car during long commutes. I learned to internalize my emotions while feeding them with food. It was a norm for me to "graze" as I thought about my troubles. My relationship with food was very unhealthy. I had no clue I was practicing the habits of a secret addict. Not me! I would never go to a party and snort cocaine, but nothing would stop me from overeating at an event, party, or social gathering. It was the plan, and I often looked forward to overeating.

Food was everything to me. I ate food because it was there! It was my stress reliever, reward, boredom reliever, anxiety management, social companion, my friend, and love. As a Bible school administrator, the shame and guilt constantly tormented me. My focus was about what others thought about me. All my life, I've mentally battled with rejection and sought comfort in food. I would ask myself, "What if they really knew the truth about me?" I preached and taught His Word, but in my own personal life, I struggled with self-control, and I even put food before God.

I absolutely loved full-time ministry. It was exciting and challenging at the same time. A typical day at the Bible college began with an early start at 5 a.m., an hour drive to the office, a drive-thru breakfast, and 7 a.m. arrival. Throughout the day, I would order out for lunch or enjoy the various dishes and sweets provided by our students. I would leave at 10 p.m., another drive-thru stop on my way home, and be asleep by 11 p.m. or midnight. My lifestyle began to feel like a revolving door "in and out." I was frustrated and unconscious to my out-of-control lifestyle. After many years of this routine, it was a daily struggle as I faced challenges of fatigue, brain fog, and low energy. I recall one morning at our staff meeting during prayer, I began to cry. My coworkers prayed for me, and one of them shared a word from God, "Francine, you need to take care of yourself." I had been secretly praying for help and hope with my unhealthy eating habits and weight gain.

During my commute home while binging on food (due to feeling anxiety), I was listening to a Christian talk radio show. The guest was an author of a book on breaking the stronghold of food. This is the moment I knew I was a food addict. Immediately, when arriving home, I downloaded the book. It is a book that, by God's grace, helped me begin to break the stronghold of food in my life and led me into a whole new way of living and eating.

On March 1, 2018, I began a new health journey.

Dreaming about a healthy lifestyle was not something I'd ever considered when I started this program. Frankly, weighing over 200 lbs for so long, I didn't believe it was possible to be in "Onederland" (weight in the one hundreds). The program consists of four components: a health coach, an education system, an amazing community, and meal replacements (called fuelings). The program taught me how to "fuel" my body with healthy food choices verses feeding my emotions. Within two weeks, I could see and feel the difference in my body. My hope was being fulfilled.

> Hope deferred makes the heart sick,
> but a **longing fulfilled** is a tree of life. Proverbs 13:12

By the grace of God, my health coach, and grit, I was finally on a journey of creating health. My journey has not been perfect. I've probably lost the same 10 lbs over and over again. Any time I'm feeling stressed, anxious, overwhelmed, or sense any other negative feeling, I **Stop. Challenge. Choose.**

Stop-Refocus on that exact moment instead of automatically reacting. I take a drink of water, so I don't respond negatively by grabbing something to eat. Just stop.

Challenge-Instead of responding with an impulse-driven bad habit, I ask myself, "Why am I feeling this way?" I question if mindlessly eating serves me. Here is where I developed the discipline of correct choice by picking the healthy response that supports my long-term well-being.

Choose-The response that supports my more important desire, which is long-term health.

Life is better 65 lbs lighter!! I love my new lifestyle. For the first time in my life, I am in control of my health. One day, while preparing a meal in my kitchen, I was thanking God for my new lifestyle, and I had a thought. . . "Life is more enjoyable when you feel good and have energy!!"

Francine Jackson
Health Coach
FrancineJackson52@gmail.com

Flying Worms

When I was teaching at The Farm, I wrote a story about a caterpillar who got lost in a bog with the worms. I eventually had it published, and it is called "Mari." It is available on Amazon if you'd like to check it out. On the surface, it looks like a children's book about standing up to the bully to follow our dreams. More importantly, however, it is about transformation and moving forward despite opposition.

God gave me the idea for the story when I was teaching about new life in Christ. We were studying the verse 2 Corinthians 5:17 about the old you being gone, and the new you coming forth. The symbol for that verse is the butterfly. It perfectly demonstrates what real transformation is. It is based on the word *metamorphosis* which means a change of the form or nature of a thing or person into a completely different one, by natural or *supernatural* means.

Sometimes, we may see the miraculous so much that

we lose sight of its magnificence. We've known since second grade that caterpillars turn into butterflies, but have we really stopped to think about that enough to appreciate what God has created in such a spectacular way? If someone came here from another planet, and I tried to convince him/her that a butterfly was once a caterpillar, the alien would never believe me.

If I just wanted to write a book about change, the main character could have been a baby bunny that grew up to be a big rabbit. The only visible difference is the size. However, transformation is beautifully exemplified in a worm-like creature transforming to something that can actually fly like a bird. Wow!

When I wrote the book, I had to cut some parts out. My picture book would have been five hundred pages if I had not. One part that was removed happened when Mari was crawling on a leaf after a rainstorm. She saw something on the edge of the leaf, and she inched closer to examine it. Her brother warned her not to get too close, but she ignored him and went up to a droplet of water on the tip of a leaf. There she saw her own reflection for the first time and became captivated by it.

"Mari" is actually an allegory of my life. Like the character in my book, I ignored the warning not to get too close to danger. My pride kept me focused on myself, not the perilous darkness below. The Bible says that pride comes before a fall. Pride can come in a lot of forms, but it is basically doing things our way and not God's. Because Mari ignored the warning, she fell into the darkness and got lost and almost died. This is my story and perhaps yours as well.

Like the bog in my story, the world can be a pretty dark and dreary place. We lose sense of our identity and don't know how to get "home." The kingdom of darkness is where the enemy resides. While in this unfamiliar world, Mari came face to face with a bully named Diablo, which is Spanish for the devil. Again, this is a picture of who is operating in the darkness. Mari has one friend named Ray who tries to help her figure out what to do, but he is just a worm with limited understanding of what makes Mari different than the rest.

While the little caterpillar was trying to survive the bog, she had a dream she could fly. Wow, that seems pretty impossible for a "worm," yet Mari was determined to figure out just what that meant. Sometimes God will give us dreams and visions in order to give us hope to keep going. They let us know there is more than what we are currently experiencing.

Like many of us, Mari didn't understand what the dream meant, but this burned inside of her as she tried to survive the darkness. Little did she know that the way to make her dream come true would be to surrender completely and form a chrysalis. In order to do that, Mari had to do something very difficult: *Let go.*

Voices of Recovery Presents
Michele

My dad was a distant person who never really made time for me. He was always helping everyone but his own family. I saw him as a good person who was out saving the world, so I couldn't understand why he had no time for us. My mom was there for me, but she had her own battles to fight. As a kid, you think that the way you are living is just the normal life that everyone else experiences, so I internalized everything and wondered what was wrong with me.

Because of my dad's absence, I didn't feel loved, valued, or secure as a child. Most young women have a heart's desire to be "daddy's girl." I tried everything to earn the love of my father and capture his attention by excelling in sports or getting good grades. For a time, I tried to starve myself to get him to notice me. His rejection was the root that produced some very destructive fruit in my life.

When I didn't get attention from him, I began to seek it from the opposite sex. One man in particular captivated me. He was 10 years older and moved into our home when I was 13. At the age of 15, we began a relationship that was on and off until I was almost 30 years old. I risked everything to be with him, and when we weren't together, my thoughts turned to him almost constantly.

Looking back, I would compare this relationship to an

addiction. I knew it was wrong, but I felt so drawn to him that I couldn't help myself. I let our mutual "love" excuse my actions, although deep down I knew that it was not right. Like an addict swears off drugs or alcohol, I tried to end our affair many times, but I felt powerless to do so and kept going back despite the risks I faced.

I believed that he loved me, so I would do anything to be with him even when we were married to other people. When I discovered I was pregnant at 29 after 11 years of infertility, I was terrified that it could be his child. After nine months of speculation, I gave birth to a baby girl that had his same color of hair. I knew deep in my heart that this child belonged to him, as much as I wanted to deny it.

The wheels really came off when this person didn't do anything to help me fix the situation that he helped me create. Dealing with rejection again, my life became a daily cocktail of guilt, shame, regret, anger, fear, remorse, and self-hatred. I felt such resentment toward this person who abandoned me when I needed help the most.

Ending my life seemed like the only way out, and I made a plan to do that yet make it look like an accident. Thankfully I could not take that step. In my search for relief and meaning of it all, I started to read the Bible. God began to reveal Himself in a series of "coincidences," and I could no longer deny His existence. Even though things were incredibly messy and complicated in my life, I felt a glimmer of hope for the first time ever.

I eventually asked Jesus into my heart, and the big knot in my stomach slowly began to unravel.

God has been incredibly faithful to me. He took that "knot" and began to weave my mess into a beautiful tapestry. I have owned my mistakes; apologized to those affected by my choices, and moved forward into my destiny. One of my biggest blessings through this situation is my amazing daughter. I am also grateful for the ability to forgive myself and those who have wounded me, while receiving forgiveness from those whom I hurt. Well, most of them.

I have amazing children, a loving and supportive husband, and it is my heart's desire to help others who have found themselves in seemingly hopeless situations. I pray my story inspires others that nothing is impossible for God. He is the best Father this girl could ever have, and He has healed my heart completely. I know that I am Daddy's girl!

Michele

o╾⊃╾o

What's Your Chrysalis?

Mari shared her dream with her friend, Ray, and made him promise not to tell anybody. I have learned that you need to be careful about sharing your God-sized dreams with just anyone. There are a lot of people who will rain on your parade and shoot your dreams down because they don't realize what is possible when God enters the picture!

Unbeknownst to Mari, Diablo had sent a spy to watch her every move. When the spy overheard the dream, he immediately told Diablo about it. The enemy called out the little caterpillar in front of the rest of the worms for being so ridiculous. Mari confronted Diablo about it, then got scared and ran away into the night. She hid in a cave for three days and was ready to give up on life altogether.

Mari was weak, hungry, and incredibly discouraged. She saw a tree in the distance and decided to climb it with the hope that if she could get to the top, she could see her home and use her remaining strength to get there. As she did this, she became dizzy, attached to the tree, *let go*, and formed a "J." She then blacked out, and the chrysalis was formed.

I was telling my story to a relative, and he said, "Well, my chrysalis was going into the Navy." Say what? That was absolutely brilliant! I could clearly see that the chrysalis is the instrument God uses on our journey to transform us into something brand new. Most people don't come to Him because everything is going right. Others will avoid God when everything is going wrong. However, if we realize that He loves us and wants to help us, we can let go and, are you ready for this, *submit to the process* that He has designed just for us!

My chrysalis was getting pregnant by one man while I was still married to another. That is not something I am proud of at all, but like I said, I was "addicted" to another person and thought I loved him, and that he loved me. It took this catastrophic event (BIG boulder) to get my attention. Through a series of "coincidences," God showed up in my life in a major way. I let go and surrendered my life to Him, and I am eternally grateful that I did!

Think of the caterpillar once the chrysalis is formed. Where is it? You could actually say it is no more or even "dead." Where it the butterfly? It is under construction with imaginal cells meeting together to form wings, antennae, and more. (What a fascinating thought and example of intricate creation by our Creator!) It is almost as if the caterpillar (old you) died, and the butterfly (new you) is being formed. Talk about new life!

In thinking about that moment where the butterfly emerges, I am reminded of a story where a young girl saw a moth struggling to exit its cocoon. The girl decided to "help" the creature by cutting open the end of the cocoon to let it out. The moth came out, but its wings never fully developed. That is because it needs to squeeze through the tiny opening in order to push the fluid in its swollen body out to the wings.

This story really spoke to me. We often want someone to help us when we're being squeezed through a tiny knothole. (Been there, done that!) Others want us to help them go through their own process because at times, it is very difficult. However, we need to be careful not to enable people, or their wings will never develop. We also need to submit fully to God's work in our lives, which in all honesty, can feel painful to the point we won't survive it. The knothole is a necessary step, and as we get squeezed through it, a lot of baggage falls off that cannot fit through the tiny space. Trust me; God knows what He is doing, and the results He brings forth are truly remarkable!

The key to true metamorphosis is *submitting to the process*. We have no way of knowing if the caterpillar is scared in that moment of letting go. However, I know that I was terrified the day my knees hit that plush blue carpeting in my living room in 1995. At that point, I really had no other choice if I wanted to live and not spiral into a deep and bottomless pit of despair.

Letting go and submitting to the process is painful but necessary. What if we were to cut open a chrysalis shortly after the caterpillar shed its skin to make it? (Of course, this would kill the creature, so I am not suggesting you do this.) I would imagine that we would see nothing but green goop on the inside. When we submit to God, He will often take us down to nothing before He rebuilds us into something. Ouch! Recovery can feel like that, but it is necessary as God begins to make us brand new. This is one of many lessons that we see in nature that apply to our lives each and every day!

One of my daughters bought me a plaque for my office that reads: *Just when the caterpillar thought the world was over, it became a butterfly.* That basically sums up "Mari," which again is my testimony. I was terrifyingly close to ending it all, but with my last ounce of strength, I moved toward the Tree of Life who is Jesus. I formed my own chrysalis and got the amazing gift of a new beginning. God destroyed the old Michele and began to recreate the new me, someone who is brand spanking new! Like Mari, I found my way home through a miraculously transformative process that began with letting go.

Before we can let go, however, we must trust the One who will catch us. I gave God my mess and asked Him to help me. I could not fathom what He would do, but His Word says this: "Now to Him who is able to do immeasurably more than all we ask or imagine, according to His power that is at work within us, to him be glory in the church and in Christ Jesus throughout all generations, for ever and ever! Amen." (Ephesians 3:20-21)

Diablo was wrong. It sounds to me like worms *can* fly! The miraculous is truly possible with God!

The Voice of Victory Presents

Juan

One day I was getting ready to run some errands before my family was traveling, and I walked into the bathroom. I had this weird feeling that I could not explain. It was like a rushing. I told my wife that I didn't feel very well and began pacing in the bathroom. I felt an overwhelming swarming of energy. This went from my toes to my head. I began freaking out and shaking. My heart was beating so fast, and I felt like I was going crazy.

For some reason, I jumped in the shower with all of my clothes on. I turned the water on cold and told myself to calm down. It actually helped a bit. As I walked into the bedroom, I told my wife I needed to calm down. I had no idea what was wrong. I told myself repeatedly to calm down. I wanted to shut down and simply go to sleep. I felt the swarm again, and it took me over, so I jumped back into the shower. I began to scream for my wife to help me. She asked me if I was having a heart attack. I wanted to call 911, but it is expensive, so we went to urgent care instead.

We were in urgent care with my three kids, and they were very scared wondering what was wrong with their dad. They asked me all kinds of questions, and I just wanted them to give me some medicine to make me feel better. I could not breathe, and I needed some relief. The doctor asked me so many questions, and then he told me that I had two anxiety attacks that morning. I told him to fix it, but it was not going to be that simple. Then I got medicine, and I questioned whether or not I should even take it. I know of friends who have gotten addicted to prescription meds, and I didn't want that to happen to me. I decided to take the medicine. I slept for four hours and felt like a champ.

For the next 36 days, I had anxiety every single night. I felt the swarming, and the anxiety felt like I was trapped inside a wooden crate. It wasn't necessarily a dark place, but a trapped place. I could see outside but couldn't go anywhere. I would have a great day, and then I would be terrified to go to bed. My wife and I would watch positive television shows before bed, and I would go to bed slowly, but it would always swarm at some point in the night.

I would run into my living room and get on my knees and cry out to God, "Heal me. Do this right now. Take this away." It would go away then come back. On day 17 I began to read a book that talked about Jesus being tempted in the desert for 40 days. I knew of people who lived with this every day, and I said that this would not be me. I said, "Lord, I ask that this is no more than a 40-day journey." Day 35 was hell. By this time, I had studied anxiety in every way I could. I would do everything to make myself feel better including drinking water, exercise, and more.

My church staff suggested going to a counselor, but so many of them were very expensive. I finally found a guy, and

I felt that the Lord wanted me to meet with him. It was both encouraging and discouraging to talk to him. I guess I wanted a quick fix. My kids were watching me freak out, and at times I even wanted to die. When I felt the swarming, I would ask my kids to leave the room. One time my son stayed in the room, and I told him to leave. My son said, "Daddy, can I pray for you?" That was so powerful and encouraging.

On day 35, I went to work, and I asked friends to pray for me. I needed something right away. The next day my friend came to visit. I could not drive more than 10 minutes from my house because I didn't want to have an attack too far from home. My friend was 30 minutes away, but I went to pick him up. I went to bed that night, and I didn't have anxiety, and I have not had it since.

With anxiety and depression, your brain is exhausted. I remember pleading with God, "I want my mind back." Maybe some of you have said that if you are suffering from anxiety or depression. I realized that God does not want to give you your mind back. He wants to renew it. God is a God of new season and new healing. He wants you to experience the fresh newness and goodness of the Lord. Romans 12:2 says, "Do not conform to the pattern of this world, but be transformed by the renewing of your mind. Then you will be able to test and approve what God's will is—his good, pleasing and perfect will." Most of us want to know God's will for our lives, but it takes renewing of the mind to figure that out.

God has us all in a process. On the other end, He has something new for us. Psalm 139:23-24 says, "Search me, God, and know my heart; test me and know my anxious thoughts. See if there is any offensive way in me, and lead me in the way everlasting." Why are we anxious? I am the first Christian in my family. Because of this, I have put so much pressure on myself to be the best, to put my family on my back, and so on. We grew up fighting to make it, and some of that is good, but I made it such a thing that it was not healthy. I also didn't get enough sleep, and it was a badge of honor. I was "team no sleep" and proud of it. Now I sleep 7-8 hours. I am "team sleep!" I pretty much gave up caffeine, where before I was drinking it throughout the day.

I felt that God was always checking up on me, and I had to perform perfectly for Him all the time. I felt like I had to grind so hard to make life better for my kids, and God was watching, and I had to show up. In reality, we cannot do this thing. We're not superheroes. Right now people are trying anything to get away from this fear, to try to heal this anxiety on their own, so we self-medicate, try drugs, get into heavy drinking, and the reality is if we don't run to Jesus, we will wake up every morning feeling the same way or even worse. We need Gods help! We get into these cycles where we try anything to take that pressure off, but it never goes away. This is a never-ending cycle that leads to anxiety, depression, or even suicide.

So what do we do when we're anxious or depressed? For

me, these things helped:

• I need to check my intake. That means we need to tighten the circle and remove people from our lives who are not good for us. I was exhausted by checking in on everyone and taking on their problems.

• Check my social media time. A study was done that social media is the number one cause of anxiety and depression. We compare our lives to others' highlight reel, and that causes problems. We also have access to so much bad news which can cause anxious thoughts.

• Check my imbalance. We have to give weight to the right things. Are we pouring too much time to our job and not our family?

• Check my indecision. Sometimes we need to make decisions. I challenge people to make three of them in a week to help them move forward. Just decide.

• Check my integrity. Gifts can take us places, but character will keep us there. When we don't operate in integrity, we can get into situations that cause us anxiety. How many of us lie and then have anxiety that the truth will come out?

• Check my imagination. That means we need to get back to childlike faith. We have to be very careful about what we are giving our thoughts to. Our thoughts can run away and cause great fear. If we take our imagination and put it toward the Kingdom, then this will give us great peace. We can reverse the cycle and put our imaginations toward worship and realize how awesome things will be when we give them to God! Jesus wants to heal and grow us.

The word "anxious" includes "us." So many people are dealing with it in this fear-filled world. When I was going through this, I felt so alone. When I started talking about it, I realized how many people are dealing with this. The enemy wants to isolate us and make us feel alone. If you are dealing with anxiety or depression, I strongly encourage you to join a church and specifically, a small group so that you can get the support from believers that you need. The reality is that God wants to heal you. He loves you and wants you in peace. God wants to supernaturally heal you like He healed me. God will heal, but it is up to us to take care of that which He has healed. We must steward our healing and not go back to old ways and habits.

How do we work through this? Is there one way to get past this anxiety? I would say there is not just one way. For me, I tried different avenues. For some it might be that you need a counselor so that you can process what is in your mind in a healthy way. For others, you have been running so hard and so fast in the name of furthering your family or growing your business, and you just might need sleep. Take breaks through-out the day, eat better, but whatever you do, don't try to do it without God. Read the Bible. One of my favorite passages of

Scripture is Psalm 91. Pray and meditate, rest in God's peace and God's presence. Do not isolate yourself; process this with people, and talk about it. Ask friends to join you and to pray for you. I am praying for you. I believe healing in this area is near. The best is yet to come for you!

Juan Martinez III
@juanmartineznow

◯━⟨⟩━◯

I'm Dead; Now What?

Hopefully by now you are seeing that it is time to stop trying to fix the old you because he/she is deader than a doornail. I pray you are starting to see that it is futile to try to fix someone who is not fixable. Jesus came to give you new life, but before He can do that, you need to accept the fact that He died on the cross for you and as you. Every gift must be received, or it is of no benefit to the recipient. We accept the gift by faith; there is no earning in the Kingdom. Believing something this monumental is easier said than done, but it is possible with the Holy Spirit as our helper. His job is to lead us into all truth.

The question you might be asking is, "Now what?" If you don't have to fix the old you, then that is a huge time saver. This revelation has been a big game changer for me as I recognize that the old me needed to go to the cross so that the new me could emerge, just like a butterfly comes out of a chrysalis.

When I was first coming to faith, there was a song on the radio called "Good-Bye to Me." At first, I would change the station because I didn't want to say farewell to the old Michele (even though I didn't like her too much). In time, I was able to let go of her and move forward to my new life in Christ. That happened as I began to know and trust Jesus more and more.

The "Now what?" question can be answered by the Apostle Paul. Before I get to that, however, I want to give a brief history of this man of God to demonstrate what real transformation looks like. Paul used to be known as Saul, and he was a very religious man. As a devout Pharisee, he did not like the fact that people were putting their faith in Jesus, and he wanted to put a stop to what he saw as rebellion.

This man persecuted Christians and ordered some to be put to death. This is a sad reality happening in our world today. Some religious sects will call for the death of Christians, and Saul was doing just that over two thousand years ago. On the way to persecute believers in Jesus, he had an encounter with God that transformed his life.

Saul heard a voice from Heaven. Saul asked who was speaking, and the reply was, "I am Jesus whom you are persecuting." (Acts 26:15) Can you imagine that moment where his eyes were opened to Jesus at the very time this man was going out to persecute the followers of Christ? Paul's conversion is summed up powerfully in Acts 26, and it is worth reading.

We know that the Apostle Paul was once Saul. He went from murdering Christians to writing half of the New Testament. That is a drastic change, or should I say, transformation. We can skim over these words, but what if a well-known terrorist became an evangelist for Jesus? That would probably make the front page of a magazine, and that is exactly what happened to Paul.

The Apostle Paul's teachings show us how to live the resurrected life in Christ. He went from a religious man who followed the rules and laws (which caused great pride) to one who lived by the grace of God (which required great humility). He wrote one of my favorite verses which is about the old being gone and the new coming forth. (2 Corinthians 5:17) His life demonstrated this truth very well.

Paul's story of transformation is also a powerful example of restoration. Sometimes we think that the Bible was written by a bunch of perfect people, but we can clearly see that this is not the case at all. Even though Saul persecuted those who loved and believed in the risen Christ, God still used this man mightily. His story is a great reminder of grace as we examine our past and realize that God can still give us a bright future in Him. No one is beyond His reach, and even the most hardened of hearts is one "Damascus Road" experience away from coming to Jesus!

So now that we are "butterflies" and no longer worms, how do we deal with the temptations that we face? Paul illustrates this perfectly in Romans 6. I would go ahead and read that right now. Don't worry; I'll wait. I would take a close look at verse 11 which holds the key to victorious living in Jesus. It says, "You also must consider yourselves dead to sin and alive to God in Christ Jesus." Another version says to "reckon" yourself dead to the old you and present yourself alive to the new you. This takes renewing your mind to the next level.

So, let's say that you were once an alcoholic. You came to faith in Christ, and the old you is dead. The alcoholic has been crucified with Christ, so there would be no reason to refer to yourself by that label any longer. However, you may be tempted to drink. What do you do? You consider yourself dead to your old ways and alive to God. In other words, the battle is in your mind.

Maybe you were a drug user and once referred to yourself as an addict. If you received Jesus as Savior, what happened to the addict? The old you is dead and buried, so when tempted to use, you remind yourself that the old you doesn't exist anymore, and the new you has zero desire to go back to anything that once had you bound. When you "kill" an addict, the addiction goes, too!

The old me was an adulterer and fornicator. I would never refer to myself as those words today because they no longer define me. The old me is dead, and the new me is a daughter of the Most High God. I have zero desire to do the things I used to do. God has filled the void in my life. I have real love and no need for the fake! Furthermore, to refer to myself as the old me which was crucified with Christ is ridiculous, damaging, and senseless. However, I see people doing this all the time.

When Paul came to teach and preach, would he introduce himself as a murderer? No, the old Paul (once Saul) is gone, and to signify that, God gave him a new name. He is no longer Saul, and he is no longer considered a murderer. More than a change took place in his life. This is transformation at its finest, and it is something that only God can do for us. In their own strength, worms will never fly!

This process of transformation is glorious, but it is beyond difficult to be faced with what you did before Jesus made you brand new. I am sure that as Paul was preaching, he would encounter people whom he once persecuted. Maybe he was speaking to a large crowd, and a family member of someone he had murdered came up to him. Can you imagine how difficult that would be?

Confronting our past is extremely heart-wrenching. People in recovery often have to face what the "old man" did, and it isn't pretty. We see people whom we have hurt, and it is not easy for us to handle. We witness the damage that our transgressions have caused, and it can be incredibly overwhelming. We can marinate in guilt, shame, condemnation, and regret, but God wants us to move forward. Whether or not others can forgive us for what we have done, we must realize that God has forgiven us based on the work of His Son. This is a finished work that opens the door to a relationship with the Father.

The Apostle Paul could definitely speak to forgiveness from regretful actions. When it came to his past, this is what he said, "Brothers and sisters, I do not consider myself yet to have taken hold of it. But *one thing* I do: Forgetting what is behind and straining toward what is ahead, I press on toward the goal to win the prize for which God has called me heavenward in Christ Jesus." (Philippians 3:13-14)

Through my experience at the Farm, I saw transformation similar to that of the Apostle Paul. I even viewed "before and after" pictures of the precious souls who went there and could not believe I was looking at the same people. I tried not to poke around in their past, but sometimes they would share their actions before coming to Christ. You could have knocked me over with a feather after they told stories from their previous life. It all seemed unbelievable, but that is what God does! His transformative work in their lives was miraculous and stunning.

I've seen gang members become pastors. I've witnessed drug dealers become evangelists. I have watched God transform heroin addicts into missionaries. I have had a front row seat to prostitutes becoming brides. I have noticed God take fearful people and turn them into mighty warriors.

The night and day difference that Jesus has made in the lives of these beautiful souls gives me great hope, and it is just evidence of what His love and presence can do in the lives of His people!

Paul's story is one of redemption and restoration. Once a murderer who became an evangelist, the Apostle Paul can teach us a lot about transformation and moving forward from the past. When you face trials and temptations, the best way to fight them is to remind yourself of who you are and who you are not. It is impossible to tempt a dead person, and the old you has been crucified with Christ. Reckon yourself dead to the past and alive to God! That is how we win this fight.

The enemy would love nothing more than to resurrect the old you and get you stuck with the behaviors that once had you bound. He will often use people from your past life to do this. He will remind you of all your sins and mistakes and try to drag you back to that old corpse. You absolutely must continue to remind yourself of what God says about you and reckon your old self dead and gone! This is how to move forward into your new life in Christ. Is it easy? No. Is it possible? Yes. Is it worth it? Absolutely!

Since I had conceived a child through an adulterous relationship, I had a constant (and I do mean constant) reminder of my sin. Days were long, and nights were filled with bad dreams. Through my relationship with God, however, He helped me to reframe what happened and recognize the humungous blessing I had been given. My daughter is amazing and navigates a touchy situation with much dignity and grace. Not only do I have a beautiful child, but this entire situation drew me to Jesus.

All of this doesn't change the fact that I hurt some people deeply. However, I must carry on. My journey has been a long and challenging road of forgiveness, healing, and restoration, but so very worth it. As with any journey, we take one step at a time as the Holy Spirit leads. Like the Apostle Paul, we are pressing on in Jesus's name! I read a statement that said, "Sometimes those with the most difficult pasts have the most amazing futures."

I pray that you will whisper to yourself, "That will be me."

Voices of Recovery Presents

Jennifer

How does a young suburban girl end up putting drugs and men in the place of God? Never would I have thought growing up that I would become a product of the life of an addict. Being curious always got me into a rough situation.

I look around at what's going on in the world today, and I thank God that He opened my eyes to see. Now I'm able to go out and reach the people God puts in my path. I have experienced what others are still going through, what people are still consumed with, and what people are still in denial of. I'm alive today to share with you my journey, which I never thought I'd get out of. All the glory goes to God; I take no credit.

I grew up for seven years with my mom, dad, and older sister, Jessica. Once my parents got divorced, my mom became a single parent, and my dad moved out, remarried, and had my little sister Julia within two years. That's when the enemy snuck in rejection and abandonment into my life. Growing up I was desperate to find love from other guys to fill that void from my dad. Did I still continue to see my dad? Yes, but my stepmom spoke death over my life instead of speaking life. I felt as if my dad had picked his new family over me and Jessica. The relationship between me and my dad was strained and broken. I was dating for the first time when my dad and I stopped talking for a year. That also meant I was unable to see my little sister.

At the age of 14, I was raped by a boy whom I've known since kindergarten. At the time I didn't think anything of it; eventually giving in. I couldn't fight anymore because I completely changed my thinking. This is not really happening. He couldn't do this to me. I must be dreaming. But I was not dreaming. Since that day I thought sex meant love. I needed a boyfriend at all times. Once one was gone, I already had another lined up. Talk about guys always wanting sex; I always wanted sex, to the point the guys would get tired of me! I believed a lie from the devil that sex is what makes you happy. Doesn't every pre-teen start drinking and smoking marijuana? That was my gateway drug to the drug that almost took me out. I didn't want drugs; I needed them to numb the pain, to keep me out of depression, to fit in with the crowd. How does a guy who beats on his girlfriend tell her to stop using cocaine, but continue to drink? Yes, mine. So considering I already believed the lie about sex, abuse topped it. How I thought I really loved him!

Two years later I got the hint that he didn't really love me, and I had to get out right away. From the pain of that relationship, I started using heroin. I had been using acid, ecstasy, cocaine, etc. This was the icing on the cake. Of course, I already had another boyfriend. As I thought about trying heroin, even though I saw what it did to my friends, I wanted to be the exception. Watch, I won't become addicted! Was I wrong! Isn't it the truth that after the second time, you're addicted? I was shooting after a couple months in secret; ashamed, confused, and embarrassed. I was in denial, like most addicts are. "Jenn, you need help," they would say. I just continued to find love through sex and numb the pain through drugs. People who live in darkness don't like the light— that was me. Depressed, lonely, and frightened, I couldn't get out no matter how hard I tried.

The things I did for drugs became a routine. Stealing from stores, panhandling, manipulation— just to name a few. How could this smart, young girl, attending Trinity Christian College for psychology, become the product of addiction? You would think getting arrested and spending time in Cook County Jail would have knocked some sense into me, but it was on September 28, 2014 that did it. Being arrested for possession and intent to deliver didn't faze me one bit. All I wanted to do was get high and forget about everything. How many times does a person have to overdose and almost die to stop using? Overdosing a handful of times and losing my life hardly scared me, but it made the people around me scared to death. No one will ever know the things an addict goes through, thinks of, and actually does, until they've gone through it themselves. I felt like no one understood me or even cared, but in reality, I know today my family has always cared and loved me.

September 28, 2014 would be the last time I got arrested and taken to jail. God had to place me there to bring me into the Dream Center. I came into the Dream Center on December 19, 2014. Since being at the Dream Center, I've been baptized, reconciled with my family, healed inside and out, been delivered, and am now employed by them. If you were to ask me on

September 27, 2014 if I would ever think of being clean for this long, I would have probably laughed in your face, to be honest. God has opened the door for a Master's Degree in September of this year for me as well.

Why do some people become consumed with the lifestyle of an addict, while others never do? I will never know, but God knows, and He uses everything that was meant to harm us for the good. Do I regret my past? No, and I wouldn't change it. Why? Because I probably would have never understood or realized my need for Jesus until now.

Jennifer Dybala

What's in a Name?

Have you ever seen a butterfly flitting through the air on a summer day? I always get excited when I see one because they have so much spiritual significance to me. I look at them and see such joy as they flit and flutter to their destinations. No longer earthbound, they seem incredibly happy and free.

When you see that magnificent creature soaring in the sky, do you ever say, "Look at that flying caterpillar!" I highly doubt anyone would do that. *Why refer to something brand new with its old name?* Read that again.

Many people who have struggled with addictions and such are now coming forth to talk about it. This needs to happen more often, and I am thankful for the movement to bring awareness to this epidemic. The stigma of addiction is lifting as we recognize that these chains have people from all shapes, sizes, ethnicities, and economic backgrounds stuck in a very dark place that feels hopeless. Whether addiction resembles a man on the streets with a needle in his arm or the woman addicted to pain pills within the walls of her mansion, a chain is a chain. Some are rusty, and others are shiny, but they all keep us bound.

I follow many people who are speaking about their past addictions on social media, and I love their stories and brutal honesty. There is one aspect that I don't like, however. It bothers me when I hear people in recovery referring to themselves as addicts or alcoholics. As I asked earlier, why refer to people who are new creations in Christ by their old name? God has given them a new identity, and it is time to start using it when referencing themselves.

Many people use old terminology to define their former selves for a variety of reasons. I think part of it is that they want to remind themselves and the world that they are addicts/alcoholics to prevent them from using ever again. Psychologically this creates a conflict in our minds, however, and that can be very destructive. Let me explain.

Proverbs 23:7 lets us know that as a man (woman) thinks in his (her) heart, so is he (she). This means what you believe about yourself at a heart level will manifest itself in your behavior. If you believe you are an athlete, you will desire to be involved in sports. If you believe you are an artist, you will have a strong desire to paint or sculpt. If you believe you are a loser, you will lose. If you believe you are a winner, you will win.

If you believe you are an addict, you will... I hope you get the point. *Labeling yourself as one thing and then trying not to exhibit that behavior makes you double-minded.* James 1:8 says that a double-minded person is unstable in all his/her ways. It is like you are constantly having a struggle in your mind. I am *this*, but I cannot do *that*.

Labeling ourselves based on our old sin nature's past choices creates a recipe for confusion and future disaster. If you really embrace that label, you actually increase the likelihood that it will manifest in your actions. The very thing you're trying to prevent is even more likely to happen. We can have many opinions about ourselves, and it can even change daily based on our performance or mood, but at the end of the day, the opinion that matters the most is God's. He is our Creator, and He gets to name His creation.

What does God have to say about this? In 1 Corinthians 6, the Apostle Paul wrote about people who would not inherit the Kingdom of God. Then he added in verse 11, "And such were some of you. But you <u>were</u> washed, you <u>were</u> sanctified, you <u>were</u> justified in the name of the Lord Jesus Christ and by the Spirit of our God." ESV

I used to teach middle school English, and I loved it (which makes some people look at me like I have three eyeballs). My students learned that verbs had a past, present, and future tense. (I hope I am not triggering anyone!) The verb "were" in the above passage is past tense. That means that it no longer applies.

It would be better to say, "I <u>was</u> an addict, but now I am a child of God. I used to struggle with addiction, but Jesus has set me free from that!" At first it may feel uncomfortable, but it will get easier in time. It is critically important to differentiate between the old you and the new you. This actually helps your brain understand that things have changed, so you no longer exhibit the behavior of the old you, who again, was crucified with Christ and buried with Him. You are then raised to new life in Him, praise God! Here is a newsflash: *Dead people don't have addictions or life-controlling issues!*

Names are extremely important to God. He renamed Jacob (which means deceiver) to Israel (which means rule with God). As Israel, he didn't go around and declare, "I am such a deceiver!" The Bible illustrates that the identity of the person is attached to his/her name. That is why it is of vital importance to call yourself a name that is in alignment with what God says about you. If you want to break free from addiction, then please stop calling yourself an addict!

Identity is critical and a major issue for people. What we believe to be true about ourselves from our heart and mind will impact our actions. Maybe we have had people speak negative things over us. It might have happened as kids, and children are usually powerless when it comes to adults speaking words that bring death over them. It is crucial in our walk of recovery to renew our minds to what God says. Trust me; His opinion matters infinitely more than anyone else's, including our own!

Maybe you're thinking that God is disappointed in you, so you refer to yourself with negative words to reinforce your beliefs. If that fits you, I would read the story of the prodigal son found in Luke 15. Most of us know the story, but the son wanted his dad's inheritance before the father passed away. That is like saying, "I wish you were dead." The father gave it to him, and the son went out and spent it on reckless living.

The son got a rude awakening in the pig sty and realized that he made a huge mistake. (Hello, boulder!) He then decided to go home and offer himself to his father as a servant. In other words, he believed that he no longer deserved status as a son. We know the rest of the story. The father saw his son from a distance (probably because he had been waiting for him to come home) and began running toward his child. The father embraced this prodigal and restored him to his proper place in the home and called for a huge celebration!

This story perfectly exhibits our Father's attitude toward us when we come to our senses and want to return to Him where we can enjoy a relationship in our Dad's house.

No matter what you've done; no matter where you've been; it is time to come home and let the Father embrace you.

God no longer refers to you by your past. It is time to come into agreement with Him and stop using names for yourself that no longer apply. The old you is dead, so quit referring to yourself by any names or labels which contradict what God says about you, His child. He doesn't refer to you as a servant. He has given you a new name. The Father calls you His daughter. He calls you His son. Welcome back to the family; it's time to celebrate!

Voices of Recovery Presents

Mary

There is only one God, and He is the God of Abraham, Isaac, and Jacob; one Savior-Jesus Christ. I never grew up knowing much about Jesus. I had no clue of this God wanting to be in a personal relationship with me! It wasn't until later in my life when this happened. I was in and out of foster care growing up, never really had a mom or stability. I was abused physically, emotionally, and sexually from family members, foster parents, and family friends. At a young age, I realized I could offer myself for money, and so I did with family.

As a young adult, I was very promiscuous with men or women, it didn't matter. I became a drug dealer and a prostitute to the world. Early on, I became an alcoholic and drug user and engaged in that lifestyle for over 20 years. My life was on a fast track to destruction in that I hurt people's lives. I would lie, cheat, and steal. I watched people self-destruct as a result of my carelessness due to drugs, or married men, or the cost of others' freedom. Some were incarcerated for the drugs they sold for me, or the influence involving others in a brothel. I lived on the edge and was almost killed at gunpoint during this time!

I had two children in my life. I wasn't a good mother. I appeased my kids with material things instead of me. I married a man who really was homosexual, and we had a child together and later divorced. I subjected my children to that

lifestyle up until I met Jesus. I thought I had everything: repu-
tation, status, sex, drugs, money. I got whatever I wanted, but
eventually came the consequences; because this is what Satan
does in his deceptions-he gives you the world, but you belong
to him. I ended up in and out of jail because of my actions. I am
a felon with DUIs and drug charges. You see Satan comes to
kill, steal, and destroy.

When I met Jesus, I was homeless, living in my boyfriend's parents' basement. (He is now my husband.) One day
I was sitting in my car and behold: Jesus took my spirit before
Him. He was so bright, like a lightning bolt! He is Holy! I was in
the presence of His Glory! The love that I felt was a love I have
never felt on this earth. In that moment I saw what I was to
Him, but also saw the terrible sins I had committed against a
wonderful God!

I was so ashamed. Jesus showed me what Satan had
done in my life, the lies and deception I was enslaved to, and
because of my choices, I was heading to hell. Sin will destroy
us, not just in this life but life eternal. My eyes were opened to
the truth about God, Satan, angels, demons, heaven, and hell.
With all my heart, I tell you it's true! All of it!

When I returned, I was completely set free from my
addictions, instantly! Jesus can do it! I remain the same today,
glory to God! In November of 2017, I was set free. Two days
later, I walked into a church and headed to the altar to confess
every sin I could think of. I shook violently and later under-

stood that Jesus delivered me of many demons. I was finally complete in peace and rest in Christ!

Jesus transformed my life by the power of His Blood. I am free from the grips of Satan. There is a real spiritual battle for souls, and without Jesus, we will perish. Today I preach the Gospel and love of Jesus Christ to others and to those incarcerated. Jesus has a plan and purpose for your life if you allow Him! I want to encourage you that no matter where you've been, what you have done, Jesus will forgive you if you call upon Him.

What Jesus has done for me, He certainly will do for you! The best thing I ever did was accept Jesus Christ as my Lord and Savior. He is my saving grace. Know that there is an amazing God who exists and wants nothing more but for you to come and commune with Him. Jesus bless you, dear ones. I want you to know that Jesus shed His blood for you. I leave you with this: "For the wages of sin is death, but the free gift of God is eternal life through Jesus Christ our Lord." (Romans 6:23 NLV) Amen.

I will always be praying for you all that you will find the love of God.

Mary Ochsner

Address the Mess

Recovery is a beautiful, messy, emotional, joyful, painful, challenging, victorious journey. There are high highs and low lows. Like any journey, taking it with people who understand and can cheer you on will help tremendously. The Holy Spirit is the absolute best cheerleader ever, so you'll want to make sure to take Him along.

We have talked about being a new creation in Christ. The old you is gone, and the new you has emerged. That is beyond fantastic news! Now that you're a butterfly, however, you will need to address the mess you made as a worm. This is probably the most difficult part of the entire process.

When I taught at The Farm, I met individuals who had all but completely destroyed their lives. To say that they had big messes and bigger regrets was an understatement. Some had aborted or abandoned their children. Others lost their kids to foster care. One woman's child died due to her drug use while she was pregnant. The stories were beyond heartbreaking. Thankfully we have a God who forgives and restores. He can help us put the shattered pieces of our lives back together, but it is still extremely painful and difficult to "go there."

On top of all that, some of them had criminal records making it more difficult to get jobs and housing once their time at The Farm was over. The world system doesn't recognize that the old you has been crucified with Christ. Praise God for a heavenly clean slate, but according to the legal system on earth, many are seen as criminals, felons, and such.

This reality makes going back into the world from a sanctuary like The Farm extremely difficult. The pain becomes unbearable to some, and they go back to the very thing that got them stuck in the first place. When we are in pain, our first instinct is to numb it. We absolutely must give our hurts to Jesus and trust Him to help us clean up the messes we have made to the best of our ability. I have seen some people move forward beautifully in their recovery, and others just get too overwhelmed with it all and go back to their old ways. This makes me want to cry even thinking about it.

Years ago, I saw a cartoon that perfectly depicts what I am talking about. It was an image of a butterfly driving a car and getting pulled over by a police officer. The man was looking at a picture of a caterpillar on the driver's license, and the caption read, "That is an old photo." How true! We may look the same on the outside, but on the inside, there is a brand-new creation alive and well, and the one in the photo is dead and buried!

It is really hard to get away from those "old photos." I know firsthand what it is like to be continually reminded of my sin. Every time I looked at my child whom I had conceived during my affair, I remembered my transgression. I could relate to King David when he said, "My sin is ever before me." This was after the child he had conceived in adultery with Bathsheba had died. God gave David and Bathsheba another son named Solomon. One child can never replace another, but it did bring them comfort and help them move forward despite their mistake that caused tremendous grief. Despite David's transgression, God still used him in mighty ways. The Father is not done with you either.

I want to add here that God has blessed me with amazing children. He took the thing that I regretted most and turned it into someone beautiful. I love my daughter and cannot imagine this world without her. She is a perfect picture of God's amazing love and grace, and this world is a better place because she is in it!

We have an enemy who loves to rub our faces in our sins and past mistakes. However, we need to remind ourselves continually that God has removed our sins as far as the east is from the west. (Psalm 103:12) Although He remembers our sin no more, we sure do. It takes time to work through this, and we must focus on God, His Word, and allow His Spirit to lead us into all truth, and that includes the truth that we are forgiven, thanks to Jesus.

Forgiveness is awesome, but the collateral damage of our mistakes remains. Some messes can be cleaned up, and others can't. We must take ownership of what we've done, walk in humility, apologize, and move forward to the best of our ability. It is not easy, but neither is staying stuck, living in denial, and continuing to make even more messes.

Owning my mistakes has been the hardest thing I have ever done. I had to confess the ugly things I did to people I loved. I had to apologize to innocent ones who were affected by my choices. I had to look into my children's eyes and tell them how sorry I was for lying to them and causing them pain and confusion. Our decisions impact other people, and that is the most difficult thing to face for me as a mom. Yes, we are brand new creations in Christ, but our old selves sure did mess things up. That is a bitter pill for everyone to swallow.

My kids and I are working through the past and trying to move forward into the future. With God's help, forgiveness and healing are possible. It is my prayer that choices I made won't have long-term negative effects on them or anyone else. I don't want my kids to see themselves as victims, and I want to break the chains of the past so that they don't infiltrate future generations. If we don't learn from our mistakes, we are destined to repeat them.

One huge step in recovery is to apologize to people we hurt along the way. Owning our mistakes and taking responsibility for our actions is critical in moving forward and healing relationships when possible. Here are some examples of wrong and right ways to apologize:

Hurtful: I am sorry that I left, but you turned out fine anyway.

Better: I am sorry for choices I made that hurt you. It must have been so hard on you. I hope you can forgive me. I love you very much.

Hurtful: I did things I regret, but now I am brand new, so technically I wasn't the one who did those things. That was the old me, and he's gone.

Better: I did things I regret. I hope you can forgive me. I am working with God to make some changes in my life, and that includes working on my relationship with you. I love you.

Hurtful: I am sorry that I was drunk throughout your childhood, but you weren't exactly the easiest kid to raise.

Better: I am sorry that I was drinking and missed so many of your events. I wish I could go back and change some things, but I can't. I hope you can forgive me and that we can work on our relationship. I love you so much.

We need to apologize and give people time. It may be helpful for them to share how they were hurt by our choices.

This will not be easy to hear, but it will be beneficial for us to understand how our decisions affected people whom we love. When you approach people, be humble, be honest, and give loved ones time to process what is happening.

As believers, we must own our stuff and not try to make excuses, blame, etc. "I'm sorry, but..." doesn't cut it. Blaming others will not help. When we apologize, people may or may not forgive us. As long as we do your part, we cannot control whether or not people will accept what we have to say. Give people time and give it to God in prayer. If we have been around this mountain before, then people may need to observe our actions to see if our motives are sincere. Again, we must give God time to work in the hearts of everyone involved. Some relationships can be restored, and honestly, others can't. We can only do our part and leave the rest in God's capable hands. He can soften hearts and work in the lives of everyone involved. Restoration is His specialty.

It is a tricky balancing act to recognize on one hand that we are new creations while, on the other hand, take responsibility for what we did as "worms." To navigate such murky waters, we absolutely must cling to Jesus's hand and let Him lead, guide, heal, and comfort. As I said before, our mess was not created in a day, and it won't get cleaned up in one either.

One of my favorite promises is that God will restore the years the locusts have eaten. (Joel 2:25-26) This means He will pay us back for what the enemy has stolen. Wow, what an amazing promise! The Lord highlighted this verse many years ago when things were still very messy, and I have held onto it tightly through many battles. Like most promises, I could not fathom how He could possibly accomplish this feat. However, I have learned that I don't have to figure out how He will, but the One who said it is faithful and true. Ahhhh, this makes my heart jump for joy!

The choices we make when we are lost seem so hard to fathom once we come to God. When we're in the world, it's like no big deal. We feel like doing something, so we do it without understanding the casualties, trauma, hurt, and even death that happen as a result. God's Word warns us of these things, but I was not exactly reading the Bible when I was creating the mess either.

Today I cringe when I see books or movies that glorify adultery. It is portrayed as exciting, glamorous, and fun. The flipside is rarely shown, however. Momentary pleasures are not worth the fallout that happens when it all comes crashing down. Decisions I made over 25 years ago will affect my life and the lives of others for many years to come. We don't always think about the consequences of our actions when we're in the moment, but God's Word holds true whether we believe it or not. I acted foolishly and paid the price for it. Sadly, so did others. Thankfully, Jesus took the punishment for me, but the consequences of my choices remain.

It is not until we see the Light that our eyes are opened to the great darkness that we defined as not that big of a deal when we were lost. When I fully saw my sin from God's perspective, it honestly sickened me. Thankfully I know the Comforter, and He helped me understand, forgive, and gradually move forward. This has taken many years, but it is so incredibly worth it to do life with Him. When I reflect on my journey, I am eternally grateful for God's mercy and grace. Because of this situation, I have an amazing child and a relationship with Him. I am in awe of His infinite love!

One of my favorite Scriptures says this: *There is therefore now no condemnation for those who are in Christ Jesus.* (Romans 8:1 KJV) The world may say otherwise, but God's thoughts are infinitely more important. For those of us in Christ, we are free from condemnation. Whether others forgive us or not, God has through His Son, Jesus. Whatever the consequences of our actions and choices, we have a righteous Judge who has declared us not guilty. When we partner with Him, He can unravel the cloak of despair and weave the threads into something amazing. I would like to believe it is a garment of praise!

Voices of Recovery Presents

Luana

I was raised in a family of dysfunction and alcohol abuse. There were six children, and I was one of the middle siblings. You know what they say about middle children; they are lost and forgotten, and that's how I felt. I believed no one loved me or even saw me.

As I entered my teen years, I started looking for love in unhealthy ways. At the age of 15 I was pregnant, three months after my 16th birthday I was married, and two weeks after the wedding, I miscarried. It was a wild ride, and it didn't stop there. Two lost, selfish, teenagers don't make a good marriage, so a year later we were divorced.

The dysfunction, rejection, and abuse from an alcoholic home created a very lost girl. Not knowing where to turn, I continued to look for that love and acceptance I so badly craved. Unfortunately, I was still looking in the wrong places.

I became pregnant a second time. I was afraid to tell my parents I messed up again, so with my boyfriend and friends' advice, I made an appointment for an abortion. At the abortion facility I was lied to. Feeling trapped, with nowhere else to go, I believed the lies. The suction procedure was extremely painful and traumatizing. On the drive home I was in severe pain and bleeding profusely. When we returned, I called the abortion facility to tell them about my pain and hemorrhaging. They said, "I am sorry you are no longer our problem, you will have to call your doctor," and they hung up. I was in shock. I wasn't calling anyone. I was taking this secret to my grave. I lay there and waited to die.

A part of me did die that day. I was angry, depressed, filled with guilt and shame, and to numb the pain I started drinking, doing drugs, and was more promiscuous. That lifestyle led to two more abortions. My life was out of control. I couldn't get out of the cycle. I tried to kill myself, but even failed at that.

Proverbs 13:12 says, "Hope deferred makes the heart sick, but a dream fulfilled is a tree of life." I had no dreams, but God had a plan. My parents came to know the Lord, and through their prayers and witness, I received Jesus as my Lord. My life was transformed. I started going to church, praying, and reading the Word.

A couple years later I married an amazing Christian man. We tried to have children but were unsuccessful. After many medical tests, they found I was infertile because of the damage done to my body from the abortions. The reality that I killed the only children I would ever bear took me on a new journey with the Lord. Could I really believe He would forgive me for taking the lives of my children, and changing the destiny of my entire family tree?

It was a difficult pilgrimage but one that was so worth it. I spent many nights crying and begging my husband and God to forgive me. After exhaustion and heartache over my sin, I crawled to Jesus's feet. He tenderly lifted me into His lap of mercy and whispered His Words of love and forgiveness over me. He proved His love for me over and over as I read His Word. During the middle of one of many nightly torments, I cried out asking for a physical hug, and God woke a friend who called and came to hold me. Our God is a personal friend and intimate Father to those who seek Him and trust Him to be who He says He is.

I have found healing, forgiveness, and love, as I rest in His lap in quiet. (Psalm 46:10 says, "Be still and know that I am God.") I have found His mercy and justice for my pain written on the pages of His Word. (Lamentations 3:22-23 ESV says, "The steadfast love of the Lord never ceases; His mercies never come to an end; they are new every morning, great is His faithfulness.") I have found laughter and joy for my heartache and heaviness when I spin, dance, sing, and worship Him in the middle of my family room. (Isaiah 61:3 says to put on the garment of praise for the spirit of heaviness.)

The way I have found freedom from the addictions, rejection, and pain in my life is to spend time with Jesus. It may be in reading His Word or sitting with Him in conversation. It may be with my hands raised in total surrender in worship, or even talking with a friend about His goodness, but freedom comes when you are with Jesus. He is the Way, the Truth, and the Life. Knowing the Truth will set you free. There is no formula, only intimacy that brings you to Love and freedom.

Luana Stoltenberg, Author of *Singing in the Wilderness*
www.Luanastoltenberg.com

o-€->-o

Birds of a Feather

We are all familiar with the saying, "Birds of a feather flock together." There is great truth in this statement. The people who surround us will influence our lives. The question we should be asking ourselves is this: *Are we hanging out with chickens, eagles, or vultures?*

The Bible says that bad company corrupts good character. (1 Corinthians 15:33) I know many people are led down a destructive path when they start hanging around friends or even relatives who are making bad choices. I am not being judgmental, but we need to be careful about who is influencing us.

When I taught at The Farm, many of the students missed their friends and family. They were isolated during the one-year program in order to learn how to walk in new life and to protect them from negative influences. Sometimes those closest to us can be the most destructive, and that can definitely include family.

I always recommended that they pray long and hard about their next steps when graduating from the program. Many couldn't wait to get back to their families to share about what Jesus had done for them. This is not always the best idea. We cannot be the saviors of anyone. Jesus fulfills that role perfectly. We can pray for people and turn them over to God, but sometimes we need to distance ourselves from toxic relationships.

This is especially critical in the early stages of recovery. As we become more established in our new identities, it is not as dangerous for us to be around others who are not the best influence. The most effective way to "witness" to people is to reveal the fruit that God has produced in our lives. We don't have to convince anyone that we are apple trees if we are full of apples.

Fruit speaks volumes. We exhibit the fruit of the Spirit when we have a relationship with God through Jesus. Those include love, joy, peace, patience, kindness, goodness, gentleness, and self-control as listed in Galatians 5. When people see this fruit in our lives, then they may want what we have. This is an open door to talk about Jesus, but again, we must use wisdom when spending time with certain people. God loves them, but they are not necessarily good for us.

The enemy will use those closest to you to drag you back to your old ways. I wish this was not true, but I've seen it time and time again. Maybe you used to get high with your mom. Perhaps you and your significant other used to have some great times getting drunk together. Maybe you and your kids used to binge eat on junk food. Maybe when you're with certain friends, you start using foul language. I am not talking about "cussing" but destructive words that speak death over your life. You cannot speak butterfly language with worms. They just don't get it.

Again, we need to ask the question I mentioned earlier. When it comes to people around you, are they chickens? Do they fear everything including the changes your recovery brings? Are they eagles, ready to soar to new heights with you? Or are they vultures, circling above you just waiting for you to fail so that they can devour you?

Of course, we want people to find the freedom we are enjoying. However, when we try to rescue drowning people, they can often pull us under. It is perfectly okay and strongly recommended to set boundaries with our friends and family. You may think you're strong enough to be around them when they are using, and maybe you are. I have just seen many people fall into traps with people they love.

I remember one girl left The Farm early because her kids were in a desperate situation. She was not ready to leave, and everyone knew it. She went home where her parents were taking care of her kids for her. They were using, however, and it was not long before this girl went back to her old ways. This young mom began to spiral down even further, and it took a lot of hard work to climb out of the pit. She was in a tough spot for sure, but we know that we must put on our own oxygen mask before we can help anyone else.

Once we travel further down the road in recovery, we can be around certain people without getting triggered or pulled back into dysfunction. I once heard it said that we should have people in our circle who are not as far along as we are, those who are in a similar place, and others who are further ahead in the journey. I think this is good advice, but we should always be sensitive to the Spirit's leading and avoid those who are not going to be a positive influence in our lives.

We definitely need a tribe of like-minded people who are moving forward in the same direction we want to go. When in recovery, people often meet with others to share and support each other along the way. I want to give a word of caution about this. If these groups are calling you into your *new identity* in Christ, then I am all for them. If they are groups where everyone is stuck and speaking negative words over themselves, where everything is gloom and doom, then I would reconsider being part of those. If you are wondering how you will know, then I would ask the Holy Spirit to tell you. Follow His peace, and you will arrive at your destination.

Everyone has a different path on this journey to wholeness and freedom. I don't want to judge anyone's walk. However, I often see people who gather to commiserate instead of speaking life to one another. That being said, we all have bad days and need to vent to people who understand. If it turns into a non-stop pity party, however, I would make some changes. You cannot expect the call of an eagle to come out of the mouths of chickens!

When I taught at The Farm, I would do a role-playing activity with those who were close to graduating. I would pretend to be them, and they would pretend to be a family member or friend that they would encounter upon return-ing home. We had some fun with this, but it was helpful to practice reactions and responses before they left. My answers as them were filled with humility, love, forgiveness, strength, compassion, and humor. These conversations are not easy at all, so practicing them in advance helped. Being around others is part of the recovery process, but again we need to use wisdom as we move forward.

We love and miss our families, but we cannot save anyone. To illustrate this point, here is a comprehensive list of everyone I have personally saved:

I hope you get the point. We cannot be anyone's savior. You cannot save your family, spouse, friends, kids, or anyone else. You can point them to the Savior, but if they are too toxic to be around, then lift them up in prayer and leave them at the feet of Jesus. (You can do this from a great distance!) Let God guide you in this process because it is definitely not easy to set boundaries with people, especially family members. No matter where they are on their journey, you can determine to soar with the eagles!

Voices of Recovery Presents
Scarlet

Everybody has a story....no one is perfect, and we all need to let go of some things that are stopping us from living the life Jesus intended for us to have. I would like to share with you my salvation story and journey.

There are three important men in my life: my dad, my husband, and my Heavenly Father. Sounds like a pretty good group of folks to be around, right? Unless one in that group is broken, or maybe all except the ONE that can restore each of them. I have chosen to share this with you at this moment for one reason, to find freedom in my personal testimony and prayerfully help you heal some broken places, too.

You see I was a daddy's girl when I was little, and I thought my daddy hung the moon! Only he didn't know how to receive or reciprocate what I was trying to get and give. You see, my dad had a spirit of rejection that ran deep and cut him to his very soul. My dad and two of his other siblings were taken to an orphanage when he was nine. Unfortunately, when my grandmother finally left my alcoholic grandfather and had the means to retrieve her children, she came back to the orphanage and got my aunt and uncle but left my dad. This was the beginning of my dad closing everyone out. He started stuttering when he spoke, and he became the little boy others liked to bully. Because, you see, they were also hurt, and they too, had been abandoned.

Shortly after this, a couple came to foster him, and for the next two years my dad would be used to work on a farm and be the whipping boy for the man who was supposed to be protecting him. So, he really didn't know how to show or give with his whole heart to anyone, especially me. This was the beginning of his "obstacle to grace" and subsequently, his children's as well.

My dad's story was not over, and God came in to rescue him from his abusers. At age 11 a couple from Falmouth, Kentucky, having only one son themselves, came and took my dad home. They were believers, and gave my dad what he had not received up to this time: a real loving family.

At 19, my dad completed high school and enrolled in the Marines. He stayed until 24, and when on leave, he met my mom and quickly married. Because of unresolved childhood trauma and the war, my dad began to drink for the rest of his life. Although he was a functioning alcoholic, he was trapped in the pain of his past.

My parents ended up having four children. I was the only girl and oldest sibling. As life would have it, the cycle of family generational sin would once more strike me and my siblings. My parents fought all my life, and even on his death bed, the tension was there. I loved my dad and he loved me the best he could under the circumstances, but for a girl not having the positive affirmations and security when young, my life started much like my dad's, and spiraled downward.

From the age of three until eight years old at the hand of my molester, life began to deteriorate significantly. I didn't want to tell anyone, because under the circumstances, I wasn't sure if anyone would care or understand. So began my season of shame; then the hiding and guilt. This would later on manifest into a promiscuous lifestyle along with alcohol and drug abuse. But God showed up when I was very young, and everywhere we moved, a church and a church family would be close by to love and support me through those difficult years.

When I was 33 years old, I re-dedicated my life to God while on a weekend retreat, and the sin of my youth and young adult life, though already erased by the Blood of Jesus, would become a real, but distant thought. I realized for the first time on this weekend retreat called "Dying Moments," that I was loved by my earthly dad (little 'd') and by my Heavenly Big Dad (God), and that we three, along with my husband, were finally made whole. The relationship I had always wanted was very real, and I now was living a never-ending story of love.

Scarlet Hudson, Founder of Women of Alabaster
www.WomenofAlabaster.org

Stinkin' Thinkin'

The entire point of this book is that Jesus dealt with the old you at the cross. This frees you to walk in new life in Him. If you are already "fixed," then what do you have left to do? The answer is simple: *Renew your mind and come into agreement with what God says.*

Imagine you worked the same job for 20 years, and you always took the same route to work. God surprised you with a better job on the other side of town. Can you drive the old way and get to your new job? No.

For 20 years you were basically on autopilot as you drove to work every day. When you get the new job, however, you need to think about where you are going. You must make a conscious decision to turn left instead of right. On some days, you may even find yourself driving to your old job just because it has been such a habit for you over the past two decades.

This exemplifies how the mind works. We form patterns in our brains, and when something new comes along, it takes some additional effort to think and act differently. Just like taking a new route to work, we must think a little bit harder when it comes to making decisions regarding which way to go. After we've been in a new place for some time, however, it begins to feel a bit more natural. Eventually, you will go on autopilot with the new job and drive there without much thought. At first, it is not easy, however. It takes some time and effort for the new patterns to feel normal.

If we drove the same dirt road every day, it would have huge ruts that would keep us from veering off the path. If we have the same thoughts daily, we can form similar ruts in our mind. What does the Bible have to say about this? Our friend, the Apostle Paul, has the answer. In 2 Corinthians 10:5 he tells us to take our thoughts captive. Our thoughts need to submit to Jesus. If He doesn't say it, we should not be coming into agreement with it. Let me explain.

Let's say that every time you go see one of your parents, he/she tells you what a complete loser you are. You feel demeaned and berated every time you visit him/her, but since this is your dad/mom, you feel obligated to maintain the relationship. Once you've been beaten down significantly, you travel that road with deep ruts, and you want to numb the pain to cope with the unpleasant situation. You may turn to a substance that helps you mentally check out, so you no longer feel the hurt of the destructive words your parent inflicted.

Now let's pull the car over a minute. When these kinds of things happen, we often try to find ways to get the other person to stop saying the hurtful words. Can we control others? No. Mom/Dad may or may not stop their hurtful words, but the question is this: What are *you* going to do about it?

Sometimes we can get blindsided in certain situations, and other times, we can predict how things will go down. Either way, we must take our thoughts captive. Let's replay that same scenario. This time you walk into your parent's house, and the berating and negative comments begin. Instead of traveling that familiar road (filled with ruts and potholes), you think to yourself, *Wow, God says that I am amazing. I am His child and deeply loved. He has a great plan for my life, and He says that I can do all things through Him who gives me strength.*

You basically counter the negative and death-filled words from the parent with the truth of what God says about you. His Word brings life not death. Like any road you travel, the first time will be harder than others. If your parent has been saying negative things to you since you were a child, then this can be especially difficult and triggering. Just realize that your parent is wounded, too. Hurting people will hurt people.

In order for you to keep your sanity and not fall into old and destructive patterns, you must grab those thoughts caused by the words of someone who should love you well and replace them with what Jesus has to say about you. This is how to take your thoughts captive.

You may also need to set up boundaries with your loved one. You can say something like this, "Mom, I love you and want to continue to come and visit, but your words are really taking me to a bad place. If you continue to speak to me that way, then I have no choice but to stay away. This would hurt both of us, so if you can avoid those words, then I will be happy to come over. I am making some changes in my life, and this would really help me."

You have set the boundary, and if your mom continues, then you have a choice to make which might mean you stop visiting for a season. I am not suggesting that you completely sever that relationship, but if you want to get well, you may have to create some distance for a time as God leads.

We also have random thoughts that run through our minds from time to time. We must take those captive as well. If you have a thought that says, "You are worthless," you must grab it and toss it out. I find it helpful to counter the negative thought with something positive that God says about us. We might say, "Psalm 139 says I am fearfully and wonderfully made. God says I am not worthless at all!" Again, we cannot help it if these thoughts pop in our head, but we still must deal with them, the sooner the better. I have heard it said that you cannot help it if a bird flies over your head.

However, if you let it build a nest and lay eggs, then you have a problem! We cannot let negative thoughts linger long enough for the "nest" to get established.

If you want to further study how the mind works, I highly recommend following Dr. Caroline Leaf. She is a Christian who studies the brain, and it can be renewed and rewired despite what some scientists are saying. She can take mind renewal to a new level!

Jesus did the heavy lifting for us at the cross, but we need to renew our minds and come into agreement with what He says. We live in a very noisy world, and we must get quiet and listen to His voice above all. This is the key to victorious living in Christ, and it is available, possible, and wonderful. If you want to move forward into new life with God, then stinkin' thinkin' must stop!

Voices of Recovery Presents

Kary

When people look at me, they see a high-functioning individual, but they don't always see my secret story. But when I look in the mirror, I see someone different, a young man with a secret past. I see that young man with a girl's name who got made fun quite a bit.

Young Kary speaks, but he stutters, even though he knows how important his words are. He focuses on the words his friends sometimes used in his childhood, calling him mean names.

It really affected me significantly back then. When my family took me to church, I felt ashamed of my thoughts because I believed you could only come to God, when you're all cleaned up. You don't come to him angry or frustrated, but you put on your best smile and serve Him with your performance.

Tragic things happened in my childhood that forced me to question God's goodness. My awana leader committed suicide, a classmate died of brain cancer, and my mom had two strokes. These tragedies kept piling up, more and more, but I didn't cope with them in normal ways.

I felt weak, so I cut off my emotions, throwing up walls around me to deal with the pain. Unable to cry, I would just suck it up and move on, suffering in silence and hoping the pain would somehow disappear. Left alone with all that pain swirling around inside my head, I turned to self-harm to cope, biting my arm just so I could move the pain from inside my head to outside my body. There was something about seeing the pain made me feel better.

In my last year of high school, I was a state qualifier for the wrestling team. This was my dream and what I was good at. Right before the tournament, I got a concussion and had to drop the team and the tournament. After that, all that was left was the school play. During practice one day I went to say my lines and couldn't get my words out. The whole cast laughed at me, and I stood in front of everyone, feeling completely embarrassed. Right there, I told God that I was done—there was nothing more He could do for me.

I felt like God could do anything at any time, but He let His own son, Jesus, be killed. And if he couldn't protect his own son, how could he protect me? I didn't feel safe. That was the first time I decided to use a knife to self-injure.

I didn't follow the path of drugs and alcohol because I knew it would lead to more pain. Suicide wasn't an option because I was too scared. I didn't know what to do with my intense anger, so the knife became my savior. When I felt the knife against my skin, seeing my pain in front of my eyes—no longer hidden deep inside me—I felt free from all the anger and frustration I couldn't show to God.

I describe my attitude at the time as a spiritual Heisman. With one hand, I pushed God away. I still served Him, but I placed the other hand over my heart, protecting my secret pain from the eyes of God.

When I graduated from high school, I started seminary school to serve Him in the best way I knew how. It may sound strange, but instead of running from God, I wanted to control Him and appease Him with my actions. I thought I could get on His good side with ministry but be completely absent from Him with true self. I needed to keep my private world and my real world separate from each other. It was a difficult dual world, and as a result, I felt tormented.

This led me further into self-injury. I believed I was an imposter who was one step away from being found out. My imperfection consumed me, and I was not okay with that. Deep in my heart, I knew that God wanted me to be perfect, but I could never achieve that. I felt that I was evil and wicked, but self-injury was a way for me to be authentic. There were deep times of anger when I was in so much pain that I would cut words like Loser and Failure into my body.

At the time, I kept myself from the Lord and listened to the enemy. At my lowest point, I carved the F-word into my body. I had so much anger, but I thought I couldn't take that to God. I believed the lie that you didn't go to God messed up until you got yourself cleaned up. If that were the truth, we would never come to God with our pain and struggles. Though I preached at a church, on the inside, I lived an entirely separate life.

I was dating my future wife at the time, and that brought love into my heart, but that also brought pain. My world began to unravel, yet I wanted to be free. I finally realized that I had to talk to someone, so I went to my professor in the counseling department.

Because I didn't want to deal with my own pain, I was afraid to go near other people's pain in my counseling lab classes. This raised some red flags with him, so I decided to be authentic with him to let him know I was struggling. I showed him my scars, and he failed me from the class. He said I was not fit to be a counselor. This was the last blow. For the first time, I shared my story, and instead of getting acceptance or help, I got pure rejection.

I believe that all sin is self-injury. We tend to think that cutting is the only form of self-injury, but we all have inappropriate ways to deal with our pain. For some, it is drug or alcohol abuse, adultery, etc. Those are also forms of self-injury that are paths to deal with our pain. Instead of going to the Father to get healing, we self-injure and choose other paths that are destructive.

To deal with my pain, I learned some excellent tools. Many people who self-injure have shared that words are too difficult to find at times. Many teens are cutting, and they have not yet learned the language to express their pain. They have all this pain on the inside, but on the outside, everyone thinks they're doing great. We desire authenticity, but we don't know how to express emotions.

The best tool I learned is to embrace a true and authentic relationship with God. Now, when I am angry with God, I tell Him. Rather than go to Him all cleaned up, now I can come to God all messed up. It is there that I find grace.

Today, I stand in front of the mirror for God and the world to see my authenticity that I've found, despite all the tragedy, anger, frustration, and pain I tried to hide all those years. With my truth no longer a secret, I've finally found safety in God, and I know everyone else can too—if they are willing to be honest.

Kary Oberbrunner
www.KaryOberbrunner.com

Roots and Fruits

When I taught at The Farm, one of my classes was called "The Garden," and it was all about cultivating a relationship with God. We found a little parcel of land and decided to plant an actual garden there. I was amazed at former gang members who would run screaming when they saw a bug or worm. We had many good laughs together about that.

The lessons of the garden are eye-opening. When we began to till the soil, it was rough going. This little plot had been ignored for years, if not decades. It was filled with weeds, rocks, and cracked soil. It took a lot of hard work to prepare this garden to receive the seeds.

This exercise provided a teachable moment for the people there. When the garden is neglected, weeds creep in, and nothing good will grow. This truth applies to our lives as well. When we are in the midst of life-controlling issues, we are not tending the garden. Instead, we are allowing weeds to run rampant. These intruders entangle our hearts and choke out everything good. One thing that we learned about weeds is that you don't have to plant them in order for them to grow. You only have to neglect the garden, and here they come with a vengeance!

Some of the residents were from rural areas and knew something about farming and gardening, but most were from the city and always counted on going to the store if they needed anything to eat. These lessons taught them about how to do life with the Master Gardener, Jesus.

One important lesson in the garden is that of roots and fruits. I would show them a peach seed. When the root comes forth, what is it? Peach root. When the branches come forth, what are they? Peach branches. How about the leaves? Peach leaves. Then finally the fruit? Peaches!

A kindergartner could follow this line of thinking, but when it comes to our lives, we plant weeds and expect fruit. It doesn't work that way. In the Kingdom of God, there is a law of reaping and sowing. You don't always get what you want, and you don't always get what you need. However, you will always get what you plant!

Instead of thinking this through, we usually plant one thing and pray for another. The laws of nature that God established from the beginning say that the seed will determine the identity of the rest of the plant or tree. In Galatians 6, the Apostle Paul explained that we will reap what we sow. It is not necessarily a bad thing, but it is a natural law and biblical truth that lets us know what we can expect when we plant something.

I love spring after a frigid Midwest winter, and I can't wait to go to the store to buy seeds based on what I want to harvest. If there was a "mystery seed" packet, I would not like it. The great thing about these seed packets is that they tell me exactly what I will eventually reap after I sow them. If I cannot read, they even show me a picture of what will come forth in the fall! Because of the law of reaping and sowing, I know what to expect.

I remember when the doo-doo hit the fan in my life, and I reaped what I had been sowing. That was not pretty. It seemed to happen so suddenly, but it had actually been brewing for years. Sometimes we can seemingly get away with things and fool ourselves into believing that nothing bad will ever happen. Eventually we will reap what we have sown. It is not God punishing us. It is a natural consequence of what we have been sowing. Plant beans, reap beans!

Although painful at the time, I am actually thankful for consequences in this life. They give us an opportunity to make some necessary changes before things get too far out of control. I know of many people, like myself, who got an education in the laws of reaping and sowing. Some of us just need to learn the hard way, but at least we're learning! These wake-up calls prompt us to seek Jesus before it is too late. When that happens, we can partner with Him to do some "weeding" in our garden. He will roll up His sleeves and help us get our lives in order. One of the things I love most about the Lord is that He won't say, "I told you so" and leave us to our own devices. He will partner with us and help clean up the garden and prepare it to plant what we really need in good soil. He is just so good!

If we continue to sow to our flesh, we will reap death. The Bible is clear on this. Sometimes we do this in ignorance, but getting a big dose of reality can often wake us up to God's truths and His ways. These things are not happening because He hates us. No, it is part of the orderly way He created life to work on this planet.

I loved teaching these lessons at The Farm. When you study how seeds germinate, there is much to learn about God's Kingdom. For example, some seeds must go through fire before they will produce life. Hmmmm, I can feel the heat on that one! Others take years to sprout because they have to spend so much time in water. My favorite lesson came from the seeds that had to go through the digestive tract of a monkey before they would produce fruit. I would laughingly tell my students not to worry. Maybe their seeds are in a pile of monkey poop, but hold tight, the answer is coming!

If you want good things in your life, then you can start by planting them. Some seeds produce fruit quickly, and others take time. The great news is that we have a God who loves to join us in the garden of life and partner with us as we dig up weeds that appeared because we neglected our garden. Then we can prepare the soil, plant good seeds, and eventually reap a beautiful harvest that will sustain us!

Voices of Recovery Presents

Tony

I had accepted Jesus Christ as my Lord and Savior when I was 16 years old. I fell deeply in love with Jesus and gave Him my whole life. Everything changed. At the same time, I committed myself to being mentored by my youth pastor at that time. He was a charismatic leader who believed in strict disciplines in life and in faith. Because of my youthfulness and my passion for the Lord, I thrived in this environment. My pursuit of God was blended with a strong emotional aspect, as is common with radical salvations.

Everything was going great until about halfway through my college experience. The older I got, the bigger life became. I was faced with a full-time opportunity in ministry as a youth pastor. However, in order to take the position, I would have to leave college. It was a big deal. After a sincere time of prayer and trying to determine God's will for my life, I felt that I should drop out of school and join this church in serving youth.

I was so excited and shared the news with my family. Surprisingly, they were not happy about my decision. I was faced with strong, emotional opposition to what I was planning to do. This conflict with my family rocked me to my core. I was in turmoil with my relationships and within myself, so I reluctantly declined the youth pastor role and recommitted to finishing my college experience. At this point, my inner world began to unravel. This was the first time my faith had been challenged by someone close to me. As a young man, I didn't know how to handle it. I loved God, and I didn't want to disappoint Him, but I also loved my family and didn't want to disappoint them either. Life began to fall apart.

Eventually I lost confidence in my faith. More significantly, I slowly lost my identity. Fear began to rule my life with every decision and every opportunity. Ultimately, each moment became tormented by the presence of fear. The enemy 'fear' is insatiable in its desire to destroy its prey. Accordingly, its hold increased on my life. This inner struggle began to press its way into every aspect of my life. I found myself struggling in such a way that it became a pattern and followed cycles of anxiety. Later, I would learn that this was OCD, Obsessive Compulsive Disorder. My life became a living death.

I struggled with every single thought. I had to wash my hands over and over again. My hands literally bled from incessant washings. I took multiple showers. I took prescribed anxiety medicine. My efforts to "cleanse" myself ended each time in futility. This reality didn't only involve physical "cleanliness" but also a pursuit of spiritual "cleanliness" which was fueled by fear and not by faith. Faith had been replaced by this new passion. A dark cloud moved in over my life. I prayed. I fasted. I went to counselors. I went to the altar. I went to revival services hoping I would get my miracle and be set free. I sat in dark rooms and tried to figure things out. I did everything I could. This journey continued into my adult life, into ministry, marriage, and parenthood. It stained every fabric of my life.

Thankfully, I had a God and a wife who wouldn't give up on me. In this striving for a cure, I would see breakthroughs, but they would be followed by setbacks. I would have moments of revelation and then other times things just didn't work out; but I never gave up.

One day, God opened my eyes to a Scripture that changed everything. John 8:32 ESV reads, "And you will know the truth, and the truth will set you free." Please understand as a Christian and as a pastor, I had read this verse over and over again. I most likely would have been able to quote it from memory, but things started to change for me when God helped me to see the full meaning of this verse. First of all, the word for "know" is a term that implies intimacy, as in the intimacy between a man and a woman. It isn't just knowing about truth or even having a mental understanding of the idea of truth. It is embracing truth into your life in the same way you would have a relationship with someone very important to you. You have to make this truth a part of your daily experience.

Nevertheless, I kind of knew this, too. And then God showed me something more. In my pursuit of freedom, I uncovered a truth about "truth" that I had never known. I became aware that truth in the original Greek language is a negative word. What I mean is that the word is the combination of a root word with a negating prefix. Just like our words, Unstoppable or Unlockable, the original meaning of the word, truth, literally means "not" and "to conceal."

Let me explain it like this. If we were to rewrite this verse, "You will know the truth, and the truth will make you free" as it originally was intended it would read, "You will know to uncover true reality and when you know not to hide, you will be made free." This awakened something inside me. What wasn't supposed to be hidden? What was fear causing me to overlook? Jesus is the truth. Therefore, this relationship with truth, with Jesus, is the key. This truth unlocks within me my true identity, my true potential, my true purpose. When I truly embrace who I am in Christ, something happens. In those moments of fear, struggle, and OCD, if I don't forget this true reality, I can respond as who I really am and not in fear.

Fear is merely the tool of the father of lies. Fear covers our eyes so that we can't see reality. On the other hand, truth opens our eyes to see what fear has caused us to forget. When that happens, freedom comes because you have entered a place of remembering who you really are. You are not dirty. You are not confused. You are not defeated. You are not bound. You are not hopeless.

The truth is that you are fearfully and wonderfully made. The truth is you can do all things through Christ who strengthens you. The truth is that you are more than a conqueror through Him who loved you. The truth is you will overcome this world by faith. The truth is you already have what it takes to be free. Don't forget it!

P.S. Freedom is always bigger than just you. My freedom has led me to helping others get free. My freedom has empowered me to unlock others who are bound by a lie and living a life of fear and struggle. Don't give up. If I can help, let me know. God has great things in store for you. You are His Masterpiece.

Dr. Tony Colson
Author of the Award Winning Book, *Unlocking Your Divine DNA*
www.TonyColson.com

○━❈━○

Root and Fruits (part 2)

In this chapter, I want to take a closer look at roots. If you see a huge oak tree, then what do you suppose is underneath the ground? Should we dig it up to see? That would be a monumental time waster. We know oak roots that hold up that magnificent tree. And all of this was caused by a tiny acorn that held its ground!

As I discussed in the previous chapter, the laws of nature dictate that the seed determines the identity of the rest of the plant. What do you suppose will happen when the Seed of Jesse (another name for Jesus) is planted in our hearts? Wouldn't that produce fruit that resembles Him? (This is the fruit of the Spirit described in Galatians 5.) If we want the fruit, then we must start with the root!

Many people want love, joy, peace, patience, kindness, goodness, gentleness, and self-control. They just don't have a solitary clue how to get it. Again, once we have the root in our hearts, then this fruit will eventually manifest. I am talking about real fruit, not plastic grapes! Likewise, I am talking about real love, not the fake stuff the world offers.

Roots are critical in the lives of the plant, but we also have roots in our hearts as a result of seeds that were sown by the words spoken over us. Life and death are in the power of the tongue. (Proverbs 18:21) Words of life spoken over us can produce some beautiful roots and fruits in our lives. However, that is not often the case. Destructive words are seeds sown that produce damaging roots, and most of us don't even realize they are there. Roots can hide very well.

Roots can tell us so much more about what is really going on in our lives. We ask questions like, "What is the root cause of this situation?" For many people with life-controlling issues, there were seeds planted in their lives that produced destructive roots. What do these roots eventually produce? Nasty fruit.

We cannot see the roots of plants and trees. They remain hidden underground. Likewise, we cannot see the roots planted in our hearts, but the fruit that they eventually produce exposes them. For example, a root of bitterness can produce some very disgusting fruit in the lives of people. The root may be buried deep in the heart, but the fruit will reveal what is hidden there.

I used to do an activity with my students where I

would bring in a big plant with many vines. I asked them to imagine that a "friend" brought it to their house. Initially this seems like a nice gesture, but it didn't take long for this plant to grow quickly and consume everything in the home. Every morning the plant would be climbing on something new. It wrapped around chairs, climbed up walls, and even entwined around furniture. The plant took over everything!

This "gift" was bad news and spreading ferociously. What to do? I pretended to try to whack it back, pull it off the furniture, and pry it off the ceiling, but it would grow back with a vengeance. I asked them how they would solve such a problem. Dealing with this invasive plant and its nasty fruit became an exhausting daily ritual that consumed their entire lives. What is the solution to such a monumental problem? The answer is really quite simple: *Just destroy the root.* Read that again.

When you kill the root, everything attached to it goes. Our lives often become a never-ending series of events called bad fruit management, and it can be absolutely life-sucking, draining, expensive, exhausting, and more. Once the root has been destroyed, however, everything that it was sustaining dies with it.

Let's put this into a real-life scenario. A "friend" brings over drugs (most of which are plant-based), and you try them for the first time. You become addicted, and this "plant" overtakes your world. You think about it 24/7. You spend all of your money to attain it. You lie, cheat, steal to get it. You spend so much time and energy trying to hide what is really going on. Your relationships are ruined over it. Your entire house (life) is controlled by the overgrown plant with its poisonous fruit that has taken over everything. It is all-consuming, and you have no clue how to make the madness stop.

I just want to mention that God gave humans dominion over the things of the earth. It should never be the other way around. In other words, plants and other substances on the earth should never have dominion over you. You were created to rule and reign over them. Use your God given authority and push it back in Jesus's name. Put them under your feet!

Again, by destroying the root, everything else attached to it will die. Like many people, my "root" was rejection. Until I dealt with that, the bad fruit it produced was never going to leave. I did not solve this problem on my own. Jesus helped me destroy this destructive root. He is the only One who can see the roots in our hearts and do what it takes to remove them. Our job is to let Him.

Jesus dealt a death blow to the root that was causing all of the destruction in my life. When He did, the nasty fruit that was attached to it died. This was a life-changing experience for me. It wasn't something that was short-lived either. To this day that root is gone, praise God!

Rejection was something that I had in common with most of the people at The Farm. Maybe you can relate. Perhaps a parent or spouse rejected you, and it has wreaked havoc in your life. It causes all kinds of bad fruit including low self-esteem, promiscuity, eating disorders, drug and alcohol abuse, perfectionism, and more. We spend so much of our lives trying to manage the bad fruit and the destruction it produces, but at the same time, we never address the root that is the source of all the dysfunction in our lives. This produces cycles of exhaustion, chaos, staying stuck, addictions, and more. All the while Jesus is waiting to take an axe to the root!

I volunteer in an organization that ministers to addicted women caught in human trafficking. The founder of this amazing ministry told me that most of the women she helps have been molested at an early age. The drugs they use are their way of managing the immense pain from their childhood trauma. They sell their bodies to purchase the drugs, and this creates a vicious cycle of destruction until the root of painfully traumatic experiences is destroyed. Only God can reach these broken places and bring freedom and love to those in captivity.

We often talk about "gateway drugs" that lead people into using more hard-core substances. The real gateway that is often ignored, however, is abuse. That is a sad reality in our world today, but we must recognize the hidden wounds that fester in the lives of hurting people. Only Jesus can apply the balm that will heal them. Nothing is impossible for Him!

All too often, we look at the outside of a person and make judgements based on what we see. What lies buried deep within these hurting souls, however, are roots of trauma that would make our blood boil. I have much admiration for precious ones who can be the hands and feet of Jesus and meet people where they are in the journey. By loving those often ignored by society, their humanity can be restored, and these individuals can open their hearts to receive God's amazing love and healing power. He is so good at obliterating destructive roots!

If you are struggling with "bad fruit," then I strongly encourage you to have some heart work done to identify and get rid of the roots that are producing them. The longer they remain, the more established in your heart they become. I can assure you, however, that God is well able to destroy every toxic root in your life and replace it with something better. Jesus is the Root of Jesse who will never leave or forsake you. "Plant" Him in your heart and watch amazing fruit grow!

The Voice of Victory Presents

Jay

I was born the youngest of 5 children. I feel that I had a pretty good childhood. Heck, I was the baby, so I got away with almost everything. We had the party house. Not in a bad way, rather, people always felt comfortable and welcomed at our house. We played cards, listened to music, danced, and did a lot of drinking.

Early the next morning after each party, I found myself so called "cleaning up." That's when I would get a chance to taste all of the different liquors that were available. I believe it all started as a little boy, I would go and get a beer from out of the fridge for people. I eventually would open it for them and sneak a sip on the way back. That was my introduction to the desire for alcohol which opened the door for me to experiment with stronger drugs.

Drinking casually developed into a habit. At first it was fun, or so I thought. It got to the point that while in high school, I could outdrink all my friends. I was also introduced to different drugs while in high school. I found out as a teenager that alcohol could make me feel numb from my emotions. Anything that I didn't want to deal with, I could suppress it with the bottle.

After years of excessive drinking, alcohol wasn't strong enough. I began smoking marijuana, snorting cocaine, popping different pills, and finally smoking crack cocaine. My father worked a lot, and therefore, I didn't receive a lot of support from him. For example, he never came to any of my sporting or school events. He played catch with me once. That really hurt me. He also drank a lot, and I was ashamed of him. My mom would say things like, "Let your brother do it. He's good at putting things together." That messed with my esteem. That made me feel inadequate. Instead of me confronting the situations, I found comfort in the bottle and other drugs. I learned about sex by watching porn. That was my idea of love. I had to learn a lot on my own. I don't blame my family. They did what they thought was right, or what they were taught.

I had a lot of bad relationships with women. I was very selfish and inconsiderate. I was often hurt by these relationships, and I again turned to drugs. I was afraid of confrontation, and I didn't know who I was. When I was around White people, I acted White. When I was around Black people, I acted Black. When I was around Hispanic people, I acted Hispanic, and when I was around Homosexuals, I acted Gay. I had an identity crisis. This went on for well over 15 years.

I was a functioning dope addict. I always had a job or two, but never any money. I didn't realize that I was destroying everyone that I was coming into contact with. I just thought that I was only hurting myself. After a failed marriage, I really started on a downward spiral of destruction. I drank and drugged so much that every day was a binge. I would shake violently and would have to take a shot of booze to calm myself in the mornings. I was addicted to whomever, wherever, and whenever. I had no self-esteem, so I would sleep with prostitutes instead of trying to have a relationship with women.

I sought help at many different drug treatment facilities, and I was arrested a couple of times. I still wasn't ready to stop. I started missing work and losing friends. It had gotten so bad in 1994, that I even checked myself into a rehab facility on my birthday, which is March 26th. I could only detox for a few days, and when released, I ended up living in a hotel. I had to walk 4 to 5 miles to work. Someone at my job loaned me money to pay my rent, and I spent it on alcohol and crack cocaine.

When I finally came to my senses, it was three days later. I went to work, and I was fired because it was my third no call-no show. When I returned to the hotel, I didn't have any money. They kept all that I had, and I was homeless. As I walked around aimlessly, I began to pray. I remember saying, "Lord, I'm sorry. I can't do this anymore. My life is in your hands. I surrender my life to you." When I surrendered my life to Christ, I knew that my life was no longer in the hands of a fool.

Instantly, the idea came to me to call the treatment center that I was in just a couple of weeks ago. You had to call every day to see if a bed had opened up. That day when I called, one bed was available, and I had just enough change in my pocket to make it about halfway there. I walked another 8 to 10 miles before I reached the facility. As I walked, I knew that God instantly removed my compulsion to drink and drug. That was April 19, 1994. It was the last time I had a drink or drug. The Bible tells us in John 8:36 ESV, "So, if the son sets you free, you will indeed be free." I now know that in order for me to be set free, I had to totally surrender. All the other times I only wanted to get out of the situation at that time.

I know I have to continue to fill myself with the Word of God and speak it over my life, daily. I must believe and not doubt. No matter what I see in the natural, I know that it is already done in the spirit. Just like a muscle that needs to work out every day in order to be well-developed, your faith needs to work out every day in order for it to be well-developed. Learn to trust God with all that you have, and He will work it out. I'm a witness that He will.

Now, it has been 26 years without a drink or drug and 25 years without a cigarette. To God be all the glory. I've been married to a beautiful and mighty woman of God for 25 years. We have two wonderful children and one fantabulous fifteen-month-old granddaughter. I'm an ordained Deacon at my church, a co-leader with my wife over the Hospitality Ministry, and we serve on our church's Ministry Team as well. Not only that, I have a catering business, and my wife and I have an Entertainment Company. We travel around to different Senior Facilities and other venues, and we perform a one-hour variety show complete with costume changes and different characters. We really enjoy spreading the love and joy of God to people who are sometimes forgotten. You can check us out on https ://www. facebook.com/evelynandjay.

As you can see, my life is pretty full. It's by the grace of God, total surrender, and trusting and believing in the Word of God. He is no respecter of persons. If He did it for me, He'll do it for you.

God Bless,
Jay K. Harris
jaykharris326@yahoo.com

⚬━⟨⟩━⚬

Up, Up and Away

Up, up and away, in my beautiful balloon…what a great song! Have you ever seen a hot air balloon? Some of you may have even ridden in one. At a hot air balloon festival near us, the sky was lit up with these brightly colored masterpieces. It was such a tranquil and gorgeous sight to behold. To me it spoke freedom to the people inside as they floated through the sky, no longer bound by the earth below.

I was talking to a friend about this. She reminds me of one of those balloons tied down with multiple ropes. If you cut all but one, the balloon is still going to remain earthbound. The last rope that would set her free was forgiveness.

Forgiveness is a huge part of life as a Christian. Jesus has forgiven our scarlet sins and made them white as snow. (Isaiah 1:18) Sin can make us feel very dirty, so that is beyond fantastic news. Because we have received this amazing gift, we are then able to pass it on to others. The Apostle Paul said to forgive others as we have been forgiven. (Ephesians 4:32 and Colossians 3:13) He was preaching the New Covenant in which we now live.

I have met many people in the recovery process who have been deeply wounded by someone. When our suffering comes at the hand of a person who was supposed to love and protect us, it is especially hard to let these things go. I have been hurt and rejected by those who should have loved me most. Through my journey with Jesus, I have learned a valuable lesson. People cannot give away what they do not have.

I don't want anyone renting space in my mind. There is a "No Vacancy" sign when it comes to thoughts of toxic and hurtful individuals. Over time, it has gotten easier to let these things go. Every once in a while, something will happen to set me back, but I am at a point of healing that I rarely notice it anymore. This has been as a result of major heart work with Jesus. Time doesn't heal all wounds, but God does. I know that He adores and accepts me unconditionally, so when others don't, I am still secure in my Father's loving embrace.

Our Savior wants us to forgive because it releases us from past hurts, wounds, and trauma. It doesn't mean that the person who hurt us deserves it; it means we do. That does not necessarily mean that we need to be in relationship with people who have wounded us. Sometimes restoration is possible, but it takes a lot of love, grace, and time for that to happen as the Holy Spirit leads.

The word "forgive" means to send it away. We can send away the offenses, wounds, and hurts of other people. We may have to send them away many times, but again, we are in a process with God, and we can turn these wounds over to Him.

Forgiveness is not an event but a process that begins with a choice. We often think that we're doing a favor for the one who hurt us. While that is partially true, I do know it will benefit us when we choose to forgive. I love the song "Forgiveness" by Matthew West, especially the line that says, "The prisoner that it really frees is you." The song was written in honor of a family who forgave the drunk driver who killed their child. Wow.

I recently went to an event where a man with the gift of prophecy spoke over me. I had never met him before, and he knew nothing about me. He asked me point blank if I was mad at someone. I responded, "Well, yes, but it's complicated." (I put it that way to excuse myself and justify holding a grudge.)

The man looked me right in the eye and said, "Why are you mad at that person when the enemy made him do it in the first place?" (Insert dead silence.) It really hit me and helped me understand the words of the Apostle Paul in Ephesians 6:12 where he lets us know that our struggle is not with people but with demonic powers. We have a real enemy, and it is not a person.

Matthew 18 contains a powerful parable of a servant who owed a large debt to the king. He could not pay it, so the king ordered that the servant and his entire family would be sold along with their possessions. The man begged the king for mercy, and the debt was forgiven. Later this same servant went to a fellow servant who owed him money and demanded it. When the king heard this, he put the original servant in jail until his debt could be paid. How do you earn money to pay back a debt when you're in jail? You don't.

The first servant owed the king the equivalent of 20 *years* of wages. The second servant owed the first one the equivalent of a day's wage. Understanding this helps us to see the significance of this story and better put it into perspective. Jesus has forgiven us of a lifetime of sin. Can we put a price tag on that? No, we are talking about our lives throughout all eternity. There is not enough money in the world to compare to being forgiven by **the** King! However, we can be like the second servant and go demand twenty bucks from people who have wounded us.

Again, we can only give away what we have. If we have received the forgiveness of a debt we could never pay, then we can freely offer forgiveness to those who have done things to hurt us. It is not easy, but it is possible with God's help and guidance along the way. If you are struggling with this, give yourself time and ask God for help.

I once heard it said that the hardest thing you will ever do is forgive people who never said they were sorry. I would say that this rings true. Being truly sorry and asking for forgiveness is a rarity in our world today. Most of the time "apologies" are something like, "I'm sorry I got caught. I am sorry you feel that way. I am sorry, but…"

The Bible says that godly sorrow leads to repentance. (2 Corinthians 7:10) Repentance means that you are truly sorry and regret the action to the point of not doing it again. That is how I felt after my daughter was born as a result of my affair. I have had people in my life who claim to regret certain choices they made, but their actions stay the same. I love this quote: *A real apology means changed behavior.* Amen.

On my journey, there was one individual that was the hardest to forgive. This person nearly destroyed my life and made things incredibly difficult for me to carry on. At one point, I actually despised this person to the point I wanted to kill her. Can you guess who I am talking about? *I was that person.* After everything I had done, I could not forgive myself. Everywhere I turned, my past choices reared their ugly head and stared me in the face. I immersed myself in perpetual guilt, shame, and regret daily. I could not get away from me and the self-loathing and fiery hatred I felt toward myself. This is a terrible place to live.

By walking with God, I learned that I could eventually forgive myself. Over time, I stopped beating myself up over my mistakes. I began to understand that the seeds of rejection planted in me as a child brought destructive roots and fruits into my life as an adult which led me to some bad choices. I recognized that as a young girl, I was powerless over the advances of an older man. That being said, I must take responsibility for my actions because I knew they were wrong. I will not play the blame game and stay stuck.

Because I was able to receive God's great love for me, I learned to love myself. This is a monumental gift. When you hate the person in the mirror, life becomes almost unbearable. You cannot get away from you. That is why so many try to escape their current reality by turning to substances that help them check out mentally and numb the pain they have inflicted on themselves and others. It offers a temporary reprieve that has lasting and destructive results.

Forgiving ourselves is a critical step in moving forward into freedom with God. As I mentioned before, forgiving others who have wounded us is also necessary. I have found that it is a process, and even when we think we've arrived, something can happen to "pick the scab," so to speak. In addition to forgiving myself, I had to release the person with whom I had the affair that resulted in the birth of my daughter. This was not easy because he is no longer living, except in reoccurring dreams that still haunt me from time to time.

In 2016 my husband and I went to Alaska for the first time. I am not sure how it happened, but I was able to forgive the man who stole my innocence and left me with the child we had conceived through our affair. For years I thought we loved each other, and after my daughter's birth, the hatred and resentment toward him smoldered deep within my heart for many years. Maybe Alaska, the "Last Frontier," was big enough to handle my pain. If I could speak to this man today, I would say that I release him, and I am okay. We have a daughter who is truly a gift and such an incredible human being. The entire experience led me to Jesus. On this trip, I entered into a new level of freedom by sending it all away and truly giving it to God completely. With this weight gone, I could breathe deeply for the first time in decades.

I have heard people teach that we are not forgiven if we don't forgive. If I believed this, then I would have gone years thinking that I was not forgiven because I was not yet able to forgive completely those who had hurt me. Jesus spoke these words in Matthew 6:15 *before* He went to the cross. We must recognize that He was still preaching the Law to Jews who were still under the Old Covenant. The cross changed everything and provided forgiveness for us once and for all.

Jesus also said that if your hand causes you to sin, then to cut it off. When I go to church, I don't see a lot of one-handed people walking around. Have our hands caused us to sin? Of course! Jesus was making a point, but I don't believe He wanted us to maim ourselves. The words of Jesus are extremely important, but we must read them in context, understand the audience, and realize that His words were spoken before His death, burial, and resurrection. The Apostle Paul teaches us how to live the resurrected life, and he said to forgive as we *have been forgiven.* (It's a done deal, my friend!)

This is a very important concept to understand. If we believe that we are not forgiven because we cannot forgive, then this will actually lead us into further bondage and condemnation because it will cause us to move away from God. I understand that we are supposed to forgive as we have been forgiven. Again, it benefits us when we let things go. However, it takes time. My complete release came 20 years after everything happened! We absolutely must invite God into this process, but if we feel that He has not forgiven us, we will avoid Him. Forgiveness opens the door to a relationship with God, and that is the goal of the Christian walk. Jesus's work on the cross is finished; we are forgiven, and He has sat down at the right hand of the Father. As our High Priest, He sat down because His work is complete.

Furthermore, if we do not recognize that we are completely forgiven and receive our righteousness from God, then we will not mature in Christ. (Hebrews 5:13) When we fail to realize that we have been forgiven of past sins, then we become nearsighted and blind. (2 Peter 1:9) The atrocities that some have suffered at the hands of others can be overwhelming. However, forgiveness is possible with God. He will help us on this journey of letting go and releasing others from the wounds they have inflicted upon us, no matter how deep they go.

In his book *Man's Search for Meaning,* Viktor Frankl

explains how he survived the Holocaust. Other people in better physical condition died in the concentration camps built and operated by extremely evil and cruel people. How did he survive when others didn't? Viktor believed that a person who can redeem the suffering will find the hope and strength needed to endure the most horrific conditions that cause great suffering at the hands of wicked people.

The only way I really know how to do that is to give it to the One who redeemed the suffering for all of mankind. He is Jesus. Our Savior endured the ultimate suffering on the cross, and His excruciating crucifixion provided the freedom for those who will receive it. Jesus is the One who gives beauty for ashes, strength for fear, gladness for mourning, and peace for despair. (Isaiah 61:3) That, my friend, is how you redeem the suffering.

My favorite part of this book is *Voices of Recovery*. I absolutely love the testimonies of people who have overcome some sort of chain with God's help. These individuals have broken free and are now helping those still trapped in bondage. This is a perfect example of redeeming the suffering. The Apostle Paul, one who suffered greatly for Christ, put it perfectly with these words: "Praise be to the God and Father of our Lord Jesus Christ, the Father of compassion and the God of all comfort, who comforts us in all our troubles, so that we can comfort those in any trouble with the comfort we ourselves receive from God. For just as we share abundantly in the sufferings of Christ, so also our comfort abounds through Christ." (2 Corinthians 1:3-5)

Unforgiveness can cause great angst on top of what you've already suffered. I've heard it said that unforgiveness is like drinking poison and expecting the other person to die. Holding onto things we should let go of can lead to a gamut of physical and emotional problems. I don't know all you've been through, but I pray that you would partner with God and send away those hurts and offenses. If you are also struggling with self-hatred like I was, I pray that God would fill you up with His love so that you can learn to love and forgive yourself.

The One who forgave His oppressors from the cross lives in you. As He was mocked and tortured on that instrument of death, He said, "Forgive them Father for they know not what they do." When you ask for help, He will give you access to His power to get it done. The last tether holding you down will be cut, and your balloon will soar to new heights! Trust me, the view is breathtaking!

Voices of Recovery Presents

Ashley

My name is Ashley White. I remember a time when I said I would never have sex before marriage, do drugs, have sex for drugs or money, or even use a needle to shoot up. Well, I did all of those things.

After being abused, molested and raped, I looked to sexual experiences to fill the void inside of me. I was longing to feel loved, so I gave my body away, all the while creating more hopelessness. I used alcohol, weed, cocaine, crack, methamphetamine, mushrooms, Vicodin, and heroin to escape the pain.

During that time the thing I loved the most in life, my kids, I left on the side of the road and abandoned them because couldn't bring myself to quit using. I inflicted pain that would not only affect me but my children as well. That created more feelings of unworthiness, loneliness, and anxiety.

I was unable to deal with my life. I felt I couldn't do anything right. I was filled with feelings of self-hate, along with a multitude of other feelings that kept me bound. I felt weak and unnoticed. I went to great lengths to prove myself worthy to others, to make myself feel better (performance).

After that 25 year stretch of living on what seemed like a hamster wheel, I came to really learn who God was. He sat me down in jail in 2015, shortly after my kids were placed with my dad. I had two cases pending and was caught yet again for meth manufacturing. In fact, we accidentally called the police ourselves. Funny, but true, and it saved my life. God was so good to me that I received Christian counseling in jail and had a reverend come speak to me every other week.

I began reading my Bible and for the first time was able to pray out loud. I began overcoming the fears that kept my mouth shut. From jail, I was sentenced to prison. There I stayed until March of 2017, when I was released on parole. I went back to my old lifestyle within three months. It was worse this time. I was at risk of violating parole and probation. I had four petitions to revoke when I was arrested again. This time, it was a DUI.

I met an amazing man, whom I'd gone to work for. I messed up my job because of my continued drug use, and he had no choice but to fire me. We were friends at first, but I knew that something was different about him. God had sent him to help me and bring me to the truth. He was a blessing in a dark time.

The pain that I was creating in him, my kids, and Dad was too great. One night I opened up the Big Book of Alcoholics Anonymous and said the prayer of faith. I surrendered my will. Immediately, I felt God's peace. From that day on He showed me who I was. I hated what I had become, I was ugly. He was showing me this so I could be conformed to His image.

God changed my lust to love. He took away the power drugs had over me. I wish I could say I stopped using then, but I kept going until He opened the door for me to go to a discipleship program instead of prison. GRACE. I married the man God had sent to me. I was married five days before I went. He was very brave to do it because I was a mess at the time. I knew that God had a plan for my life. I continued challenging every thought and belief I had about people and myself that were all based on my past. God was awakening me to His love.

God isn't finished yet! In June our children will come home to live with us! I see God at work in my children through the obedience and teaching that we are providing. God has opened the door for me to work at the Chicago Dream Center (The Farm). This is the discipleship program I went to for a year. They really are more like a family. I also see God's hand over my mother's life. She and I used together, and through prayer, the Lord is bringing her to where she is destined to be. God is also teaching me how to be a godly wife. This is sometimes harder than you think. No matter what, I am grateful for the Lord for showing me how to walk out this new life!

God's love has the power to break off everything. I owe my life to Him for now restoring our children to us. He is giving me dreams of my future and opening my eyes that were once blinded. What God does in our lives when we come into obedience to Him is more than you or I could ever fathom. I pray that you would receive this gift of love. And I pray that you, being rooted and established in love, may have power, together with all the Lord's holy people, to grasp how wide and long and high and deep is the love of Christ, and to know this love that surpasses knowledge-that you may be filled to the measure of all the fullness of God. (Ephesians 3:17-19) In Jesus's name.

Ashley White
ashleywhite@phoenix-restoration.com

Time for Me to Fly!

I love that song by REO Speedwagon…Oh, I'm gonna set myself free. Flashback to 1981 as I cruised down the highway in my pumpkin orange MGB, but I digress. I want to get back to my picture book and share an important reason that I wrote "Mari" in the first place, and it hits very close to home.

Once Mari emerged from her chrysalis, all the pieces of the puzzle came together for her. She remembered the butterflies that laid eggs on the milkweed plants, and she recognized that she had become one. Her dream had come true, and she announced it to the world. Mari was not crazy after all. She became a brand-new creation with long legs and silky wings!

At that point in the story, the enemy returned. (Insert dramatic music that lets you know he's baaaaack.) Ray pointed out to Diablo that Mari was right, (and he was wrong).

Diablo glanced up at the butterfly and said that he didn't know who was on the tree branch, but he knew it was not Mari.

Okay, let's park the car right here. This is the culmination of everything that happened and the big moment in the story. Let me explain. When I taught at The Farm, the people there were excited about their new identity in Christ, and they were ready to show off their "wings" to the world. That often included family members. They could not wait to get home to their spouse/children/parents and tell everyone about their amazing transformation through a newfound relationship with Jesus.

Some families were truly joyful that their loved ones had gotten a fresh start. Many had been praying that they would be able to break free from the life-controlling issues that once had them bound. That was not always the case, however. Many times, these people would be faced with their own Diablo who didn't recognize the metamorphosis from "worm" to butterfly that had occurred.

This truth is always heartbreaking for me, not to mention those that experienced it. They were confronted with comments like, "Who do you think you are? You look like the same old _____ to me. You haven't changed a bit!"

Now why would anyone say something so cruel? The Bible says that the natural mind *cannot* understand the things of God. (It did not say *will* not.) If you haven't experienced transformation yourself, it's very difficult to see it in someone else. If family members have their own life-controlling issues, then maybe they denied the transformation to keep themselves protected from having to admit that real change is possible. Boom!

For whatever reason, some faced terrible opposition when they returned home. We so desperately want affirmation from loved ones when we accomplish something fantastic like getting clean, breaking free from the past, and moving forward into the future. I wrote this part into the story, "Mari" because I lived it myself, and it was not pretty.

As I mentioned previously, I was unfaithful to my first husband and conceived a child that was not his. That is a despicable thing to do, and I was truly repentant for my actions. I tried desperately to bury my secret for years and cover up my horrible actions with many lies. I felt so much shame as what I had done was so deceitful and awful. Eventually I gave my life to God and invited Jesus into the huge mess I had created.

Like many secrets, mine was discovered, and I eventually got a divorce. It was all very ugly and traumatic for me and my entire family. God had transformed me from an "adulterer" to a daughter of the Most High God. I was once a "worm" who did worm-like things, but that old me had been crucified with Christ. I emerged from my "chrysalis" as something brand new. This took me years to work through, but I finally forgave myself and embraced the blessings in disguise that were before me. However, I had to take responsibility for the mess I made as a "worm." I had to apologize, confess, and try with everything I had to make amends. For the sake of my kids, I had to press on.

Well, my "Diablo" didn't accept the new me. He wanted me to crawl over broken glass the rest of my life and pay for what I had done. My children got caught in the crosshairs of this, and it was a huge and painful mess that I helped to create. I tried and tried to convince a certain person that I had been transformed, but to an unbeliever, that sounds like a great big copout to excuse bad choices.

I knew what these individuals at The Farm were going through when their Diablo didn't applaud their transformation. Here is where the rubber hits the road. If they are waiting for a thumbs up, applause, or "way to go" from certain people, it may never happen. *If it does, great. If it doesn't, move forward anyway.* Read that again.

Mari could have stayed on the branch until Diablo affirmed her, told her she was right about her dream, and gave her a standing ovation for becoming a butterfly. Guess what? She would have stayed stuck, with wings, and I see it happen all the time. If God did it, and you know it, then move forward into your destiny with Him no matter what the naysayers and haters say!

I am going to share a sad reality that many do not

want to hear. Some people don't want to recognize the transformation in you, and others actually want you to go back to your old life. If friends or family members are stuck in their own messes, then seeing you get out of yours lets them know that freedom is absolutely possible. Many want to live in a world which says no one can change; things stay the same; this is how we do things; it's been in the family for years, etc. Some may even go to great lengths to sabotage your recovery. I am back to the question I started with in this book: *Do you want to get well?* If the answer is yes, then you must do *whatever it takes* to move forward into your destiny with God. If that means cutting certain people out of your life, then I'll hand you the scissors!

We want to take everyone with us on our journey to freedom, and some refuse to board the train. What we *can do* is pray for people, love them, and show them what is possible with God. Remember that you cannot save loved ones, but you can leave them at the foot of the cross in prayer. Sometimes you must let go and move on anyway. That is difficult, but so is staying stuck. Reminding ourselves of how stubborn we once were can help us show compassion to those who don't want to receive what God has freely given them…yet. Some may never want to hear what you have to say, and others are simply not ready. I could preach on that!

Shortly after I got saved, I went to two family members to share my testimony. (I gave the "G" rated version at the time because I was not going to tell anyone my big secret.) I felt like my words left my mouth and went thud on the floor with no response. About seven years later, one of those individuals said that when I shared my story, it was the beginning of his return to faith in Christ. Say what? It took seven years to get any kind of affirmation that my words made a difference. It reminds me of this quote: *You cannot force people to comprehend a message they are not ready to receive, but never underestimate the power of planting a seed.* We plant seeds, but God makes them grow!

Some people need to go through their own process with God before they will surrender to Him. Others are indifferent and may never come to faith. Then there are those who will actually persecute you for your faith. I saw something on social media that summed up my feelings on this perfectly: *People don't recognize the new you because they are still the old them.* Bam! There is not enough ink in my highlighter to do justice to that statement!

Mari wanted Diablo to recognize her in the transformed state. When he continued to mock her, she looked at the worm with fresh eyes. She realized he wasn't mean; he was afraid. That's right; the enemy is afraid of your potential in Christ. Once you know who you are, you know who you aren't. The old you is dead and buried, and the new you has been resurrected to new life in Christ. Wow, that is such a beautiful, powerful, and amazing truth!

I remember a time when I tried to convince my Diablo that I had transformed into something new. He would have none of it. I wrote letters and talked until I was blue in the face to no avail. When I finally believed who I was in Christ, then I stopped trying to convince him of my transformation. In that moment, I learned that I was not really trying to convince him; *I was actually trying to convince myself.* Once I believed it to be true, I quit arguing with my accuser. You know what? He stopped saying those negative words against me. I learned that it is not fun to argue with someone who refuses to engage!

"Mari" is my story. My foolish pride caused me to tumble into the darkness. I got lost and didn't know who I was or how to get out of the mess I found myself in. I had a dream that things could be different, but I could not comprehend how. I nearly gave up but came to Jesus instead. I let go and submitted to the process. He transformed me into something brand new. I broke free from my past and now have an amazing future. I am truly enjoying my flight which is taking me to incredible destinations!

Like Mari, I have also faced the enemy and realized he is afraid of me. He is terrified of everything I am becoming in Christ. The devil is scared that I will take back territory that was stolen from me. My adversary is petrified that I will help others find freedom with my story and the testimonies of others. I guess he should be afraid because that is precisely what I am doing! Praise God Who made it all possible!

In the end, Mari decided to take flight. It was time to leave her wormy past behind and move forward to new adventures as a butterfly. Despite the negativity that Diablo threw her way, she launched into her future with the wind (Holy Spirit) guiding her to new adventures with Him. Your wings are ready, my friend. It's time for **you** to fly! The end is just a new beginning. Like me, I pray you will enjoy your flight as you soar to new heights with Jesus!

Voices of Recovery Presents

Cody

I grew up as a third-generation drug dealer and user. Both my parents were addicted and not really around my life much. I saw drug use and activity from my parents and grandparents on both sides. It was in every part of my family. When I saw what it did to my parents and relatives, there was something in me that despised drug use. I told myself that I would never use or become addicted. I ultimately became the very thing that I hated because part of it was generational.

My dad went to prison for selling drugs when I was 9. I started using when I was 12, and I tried every drug you can imagine. I started dealing at the age of 14. I didn't have any background in church, and I hung out on the streets. That is who my family was. It where I found what I thought was love and loyalty. A lot of my friends have similar stories of coming from single parent homes and chaotic backgrounds.

I don't remember hearing about God growing up. I might have been to church once as a kid, but it was just to eat pizza and hang out. I had no background spiritually. When I was 19 my dad got out of prison. He started selling heroin and pills, and I helped him do it. He was supplying me, and that is when I got addicted to opiates which led to my heroin addiction. I used from the ages of 12 to 24.

Shortly after my dad got out of prison, he got radically

saved. I didn't know much about church, and I knew he was facing the possibility of going back to prison. The only thing I knew about it was like a rap song said that if you're scared, you go to church. I figured he was scared to go back to prison and therefore going to church. After about 30 days, I realized some real transformation had taken place in his life.

My dad invited me to go listen to him speak at a homeless shelter in our hometown. The message was spoken to everyone but geared toward me. He said he didn't want me to see him as his hero, but that Jesus should be my hero. That day I gave my heart to Jesus. I confessed Him with my mouth, but I didn't really know what I was getting myself into to be honest. I prayed a prayer and meant what I said, but I was not ready to depart the lifestyle I was living.

From that day on, I battled being a Christian. I spent the ages of 19 to 24 in a whirlwind. I'd be good for a few months then start using and go back to jail. In my opinion, I was the worst example of a Christian you could ever see. I could quote Bible verses and be high on heroin at the same time. I was a religious drug addict who tried to stuff my mind with God instead of letting Him fill my heart. I won't deny that I had an encounter with God, but I didn't continue in it. I thought the more I knew, the better off I would be. To be honest, it wasn't about what I knew but Who I knew. I didn't know Jesus the way I thought I knew Him. I just knew He was real.

I started going into rehab at the age of 15. I came back to

Heritage House when I was 24, and it was my 10th rehab. I basically went to rehab every year from the ages of 15 to 24. Going back there was the last thing I wanted to do. I didn't want to be part of community living, but I knew if I didn't do something, I would be strung out in no time. At this point in my life, I had been a Christian for about five years. I had been used in ministry, preached, been in youth leadership, and I wanted to go to Bible college. I had an opportunity to get my probation transferred and go to Bible college in Florida. God had other plans.

God spoke to me and said that one of the reasons I had so much trouble was that I was not willing to finish anything I had started. I told Him that if I never get to do the things that I thought I was called to do, then I would be okay. One of those things was to go to Bible college. I told Him that I would not go to Bible college if He wanted me to stay at Heritage House. Going to Bible school or being around addicted people? No one in their right mind would choose to go back into a rehab facility. Well, it wasn't about what I wanted but what He wanted me to do. They called and said I could go to Bible college, and I didn't do it. That was the end of that.

I spent 18 months at Heritage House. It became different this time. Throughout my life, I was always able to be a role model student and shining star. I could modify my behavior to get by. I could say the right words and do the right things. In my heart, I genuinely meant it. The problem was I had never been discipled in my life. I never allowed anyone in my life who would tell me no. I did what I thought was right even if it wasn't. This time I had to put my life into the hands of other people and quit trusting myself. This was not easy. It became about the state of my heart.

My heart was dirty. I loved God, but I was sick. I admitted that I had hidden sin in my life. It was easy to get off drugs. I could get off of them within weeks, but that is not what my real problem was. It was the hidden things in my heart, and I was afraid that if people found out these things about me, then they would not want anything to do with me. What happened is that God began to speak to these things in my life. He began to expose lust, sexual perversion, manipulations, and such that I had lived with my entire life. It kept me from developing character and being the man God wanted me to be. I thought, "When people find out who I really am, they will want to get rid of me." I believed it would be too much to deal with. That is why I tried to keep everything hidden.

I found that through the people I met at Heritage House, I had found a family. I didn't just find a program. These men became spiritual fathers in the faith to me. The reason they didn't kick me to the curb is that they treated me like I was their own son. They held me to a standard, but they also helped me walk through difficult areas of my life and conquer them. It is only through the grace of God that He sent men like that into my life to help. That is what people in addiction need. It's not an easy thing because we've done everything under the sun to get clean, but it is not just about praying a prayer.

People don't get fixed by praying a prayer. It is a process of that God must walk you through. I graduated the program in 10 months. There were only four people here at that time. Then I did the internship and was there a total of 18 months. Then I got hired at the church and transitioned me back to manage Heritage House, the place where I found freedom myself.

God is blessing me throughout what I do. I didn't think I was qualified to do it, but He told me to do it. Our facility has grown to 75 men. I have seen so many miracles take place. One is that my dad is still clean and serving God. We have a great relationship today, and he loves what is happening in my life. My mom saw what I was doing and decided to get treatment in a faith-based discipleship program, and she is serving the Lord. I am reconnecting with my sister who is also serving God. It is like He shifted my entire family just based off a seed of faith that was planted in the ground that began to break off generational curses from my family.

I am helping guys that I have known for over 10 years. These are the guys I used to hang with and use drugs around. When I said yes to God, there began to be a domino effect to everyone who was connected to me even from my past. I am literally seeing miracles take place on a daily basis. Every day I get to see guys' lives being transformed by God's love and presence.

God told Moses to tell the people that for those who do not obey Him and His commands, their iniquity will be visited to their children to the third and fourth generations. But if people will love and obey Him, then the generational blessing will be passed down to a thousand generations. What you realize is that what determines the curse or the blessing over someone's life, is their response to God. Are you going to do what God says or do what you want? If you begin to do what God says, the things that used to kill you will begin to fall off your life and will not be passed to future generations.

I am married, and I have a stepdaughter and a baby. My kids will never have to go through what I went through because I made a decision for God to change my life. My wife used to be an alcoholic. God can take the most broken things and make them into trophies. It reminds me of the caterpillar. The moment it thought its life was over, it turned into a butterfly. This is what we see that through the redemption of Jesus, we are caterpillars in the cocoon of His presence. When we think everything in our life has come to an end, and it's just a heap of ashes, then God literally transforms us into something brand new.

In the end, I realize I was not addicted to drugs but to myself. I have now switched my addiction. I am now addicted to God, to helping addicts, to God's presence, and to supernatural events and miracles that take place every day. I have learned to live broken and humble before God, and I tell Him whatever He wants to do, I will do. I will not force my hand with Him. I would not change what I am doing unless He asked me to. That is the only way I know to live this life.

Cody Jones
Manager at Heritage House
www.CityonaHill.com/Heritage-House
www.HopeoverHeroin.com

Epilogue

The first time I shared my story at The Farm, I had such a sense of overwhelming peace, relief, and gratitude. I was nervous at first, but I realize that sometimes courage is doing it afraid. There was a time I swore I would never tell a living soul my secret, but that was a heavy burden to bear. Buried things usually work their way up to the surface, and I am now thankful that they do.

After I gave my testimony, I had a cleansing cry, then several of my students came up and shared ways they could relate to what happened to me. Some of them had children by men they were not married to. Some of them were the children conceived in an adulterous relationship. Most of them had been rejected by family members. On many levels, they could connect to what I had shared. Above all, my story gave them hope that God could turn their mess into a message just like He has done for me.

Years ago, I had the opportunity to share my testimony with someone very close to me. He said, "I don't see you any different." That man is now my husband, and when I was able to find the strength to share my darkest secret with him, he didn't flinch. To hear those words of affirmation after all I had been through was pure gold. I knew he was the one for me.

It's time to land this plane, and I am so excited for the journey you have embarked upon. I know what Jesus can do with a surrendered heart. He is so good! I never in my wildest dreams imagined this life I am living now. I have a beautiful family which includes a wonderful husband who loves and supports me. I have my mom who is my biggest cheerleader. I've been incredibly blessed with amazing children and grandchildren. I have a front row seat as God restores broken hearts and wounded relationships. I am eternally grateful for His amazing and redeeming love!

By His grace, I love God, myself, and others. Believe it or not, I actually have come to the place where I absolutely can embrace and appreciate my journey with all of the valleys and mountaintops included. As the song says, "Sometimes a rough and a rocky road leads you to a beautiful place." It is my deepest desire that it can encourage someone that all things are truly possible with God. After all, He turns worms into butterflies.

Flying,
Michele

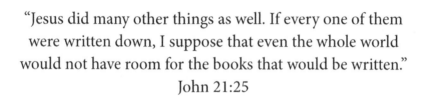

"Jesus did many other things as well. If every one of them were written down, I suppose that even the whole world would not have room for the books that would be written."

John 21:25

You have read some amazing stories of real people who have gotten through some extremely difficult circumstances with God's help. The Bible says that we overcome by the blood of the Lamb and the word of our testimony. (Revelation 12:11) We take what Jesus did for us and apply it to our lives. We make it personal and share it to encourage others who need the hope of the Gospel.

Now it is your turn. Take some time to write down what the Lord has done for you. Remember, we are all in a process with God. Be encouraged with these words: *He who began a good work in you is faithful to complete it.* (Philippians 1:6.) I hope to be able to read your story someday. If not in this life, look me up in Heaven, and we can marvel in all God has done for us!

Voices of Recovery Presents

Your Name:_____

Guest Speaker

Michele Eich

www.20VoicesofRecovery.com

Author, Speaker, Growth
Coach, Minister

Michele Eich is a passionate and dynamic speaker who loves to see Jesus set the captives free. She knows that nothing is impossible for God! As a certified growth coach and minister, Michele encourages people to move forward into God's love, presence, and power.

She will have audiences laughing one minute and crying the next by sharing stories of real-life overcomers. Michele has her own redemption story and wants to help people walk into their destinies with God.

Topics:
- Overcoming obstacles
- What gets us stuck and unstuck
- Identity as Sons and Daughters of God
- How to get off the "hamster wheel"

Great for:
- Keynote
- Church Services
- Conferences
- Retreats
- Podcasts

Contact Michele

Website 20VoicesofRecovery.com
Email 20VoicesofRecovery@gmail.com
Facebook www.facebook.com/20Voicesof-Recovery

Tune in to Michele's weekly show,
Voices of Recovery on Facebook!

Made in the USA
Coppell, TX
08 June 2022

78590924R00125